Stormy Seas

Understanding God in the Midst of Life's Tempests

WENDY ARMFIELD

Nampa, Idaho | www.pacificpress.com

Cover design by Gerald Lee Monks
Cover illustration supplied by author.

Copyright © 2021 by Pacific Press® Publishing Association
Printed in the United States of America
All rights reserved

The author assumes full responsibility for the accuracy of all facts and quotations as cited in this book.

Unless otherwise noted, all Scripture quotations are from the New King James Version®. Copyright © 1982 by Thomas Nelson. Used by permission. All rights reserved.

Scripture quotations marked AMP are from the Amplified® Bible, copyright © 2015 by The Lockman Foundation. Used by permission. (www.Lockman.org)

Scripture quotations marked KJV are from the King James Version of the Bible.

Additional copies of this book are available by calling toll-free 1-800-765-6955 or by visiting http://www.adventistbookcenter.com.

Library of Congress Cataloging-in-Publication Data

Names: Armfield, Wendy, author.
Title: Stormy seas : understanding God in the midst of life's tempests / Wendy Armfield.
Description: Nampa, Idaho : Pacific Press Publishing Association, [2021] | Includes bibliographical references. | Summary: "A study on how God led His children through trials in the Bible, and how we can apply the lessons to our lives today"— Provided by publisher.
Identifiers: LCCN 2021001777 | ISBN 9780816367542 (paperback) | ISBN 9780816367559 (ebook)
Subjects: LCSH: Trust in God—Biblical teaching. | Providence and government of God—Biblical teaching. | Faith—Biblical teaching.
Classification: LCC BV4637 .A66 2021 | DDC 231—dc23
LC record available at https://lccn.loc.gov/2021001777

January 2021

Dedication

I want to dedicate the creation of this book to my Friend and Savior, Jesus Christ. This book is a collection of lessons He has taught me as I searched for Him and sought to understand Him during life's storms.

Jesus has revealed to my searching heart adequate answers to most of my questionings. And what has not been revealed, clearly understood, or presented for study in God's Word, I can let go. I can do this because what I have learned about God in His Word has given me plenty of confidence to trust Him with the things I cannot know.

Thank You, Jesus!

Contents

Foreword		7
Preface		11
Introduction		15
Chapter 1	A Disrupted Journey	17
Chapter 2	Plan and Promise	24
Chapter 3	Peace and Trouble	28
Chapter 4	Provision and Promise	35
Chapter 5	Bread From Heaven	42
Chapter 6	The God Who Sees Us	49
Chapter 7	The Good Shepherd	57
Chapter 8	In the Fire	66
Chapter 9	When the Path Ends	72
Chapter 10	Decisions and Consequences	77
Chapter 11	The Meaning of "God With Us"	82
Chapter 12	A Surprising Time to Thrive	88
Chapter 13	In the Dungeon	91
Chapter 14	Forgotten and Forlorn	101
Chapter 15	Wait on the Lord	107
Chapter 16	In His Power, Amen!	118

Foreword

When Wendy asked me whether I would consider writing the foreword to her book, I had to grab the side of my desk to keep my balance. I had the privilege of reading each chapter as she finished them, and I was fascinated with her ability to bring fresh insights to these familiar Bible stories and take me into God's very presence.

Through the years, I have come to know Wendy's heart. She is truly one of our Abba's ambassadors here on this dark planet. I love the way her mind works. She takes Scriptures and talks to God about them and puts them together in beautiful blends that create lovely new insights and understandings. I can only imagine the fun she will have throughout eternity when the twists and zigzags that exist here now are forever gone. She will be in her element—truth in all of its purity and beauty.

So do you wonder what the truth is about the constant onslaught of problems and heartaches as we journey through our lives? I remember being told as a young person with an alcoholic mother that if I would just give my heart to Jesus, He would make everything right. Well, it didn't happen. No smooth sailing for me!

So, again, do you wonder, along with myriads of other struggling people, what the answer is to the question of why bad things happen to good people?

Actually, I will reframe that question: Why does God permit bad things to happen to the people He created—in particular to those who have given themselves to Him?

"Trust in the Lord with all your heart"

I am a slow learner, it seems. I did not know much about God until I was well into adulthood. By then, I had formed some unhealthy habits and attitudes and decisions that *seemed* to help me cope with some of the traumas in my life—physical and emotional abuse, feelings of being unloved and alone, and a sense of being completely inadequate to change or improve anything.

But you know what? Our God is such a wise, compassionate Father and Friend. He knew just how to lead me into a deeper truth about Him. Because, you see, one of the unhealthy opinions I had made about God was that He was angry because of all of my failures in trying to conform to His standards.

The pictures that Wendy paints for us in *Stormy Seas* are of a God, the true God, whose mercy and sensitive love for each of us are as endless as eternity. And that is one thing I am gradually learning. Trusting in His very personal love for *me* is a warm and wonderful comfort.

"Lean not on your own understanding"

Learning to lean on God rather than on my own understanding has been a challenge. I find that it is not a one-time thing; it is an ongoing process—a process that has required (at least for me) much repetition. When I decide to do something, the first thing in the process is to begin. So I begin and move along, and suddenly, an interruption occurs. Someone or something interrupts. A person needs something, a machine malfunctions, or an icy storm prevents travel. *Then*, oh yes! Then I arrive at a choice point. When I remember that my Lord is in control of everything—*everything*, even the interruptions—then I can decide to lean on Him. But so often I take that interruption as a frustrating event, and my own understanding shatters into anxiety, anger, or discontent.

"In all your ways acknowledge Him"

When I turn all of my affairs over to God's control and acknowledge Him as Lord of my life, I can rest—truly rest. This universe, with all its workings and upkeep, is under the control of the One who wants me to be His trusting child. The Lord's wisdom, understanding, and knowledge are as far above mine as the remote edges of the universe are beyond my reach. When I acknowledge that from a worshipful heart, His peace and joy flood my soul—even in the middle of life's many interruptions.

"He shall direct your paths"
It has been said that people can be divided largely into two camps: those who think they can, and those who insist they can't. Both are wrong, and both need divine help.

Both camps need a loving Father to guide their steps in the path that leads to Him. Psalm 23 tells us that this path of righteousness leads through some beautiful country—through green pastures and beside still waters. But it also leads through dark valleys of death and right into the midst of enemies.

In Revelation 3:20, Jesus tells us that He is standing at the door to our heart, and He is knocking. He will not just barge in. No, the enemy does that but not our heavenly Father. He respects the choices we make. But He has promised that if we hear His voice and open the door, He will come in and dine with us, fellowship with us, and share His wisdom and guidance. As we acknowledge Him and follow His leading, regardless of what situation we find ourselves in, *that* is the very place where God is waiting for us to meet Him. Our compassionate Father is waiting to provide us with nourishing strength, hope, and guidance.

There is one final thing: I want to tell you how I know Wendy Armfield. She lives quite a few miles from me on a rugged mountain with her husband and their beloved feline "kids." Nearby are her husband's parents. Wendy's parents live on another mountain fairly close by in a charming log cabin they built when her older sister was just a toddler. The girls grew up there, hiking and riding their horses through the valleys and over the hills, drinking in the beauties found only in the Rocky Mountains. Wendy's mom is one of my dearest friends. We have known each other for years, actually since she was born. You see, Wendy's mom is my oldest daughter. So, of course, it follows that I am honored and very happy to have Wendy as one of my granddaughters.

I invite you to go with Wendy deeper into the lives of some people who have personally experienced remarkable interactions with their Maker. He will use anything in our lives, if we turn it over to Him, to reveal to us our personal soul sickness so that we can surrender it to Him for healing.

Travel with Wendy, and let God's Spirit guide your journey. I join my prayers with hers as you explore your own very personal walk with our amazing God and discover the rich stores of joy and peace and power He is longing to share with you.

Trust in the LORD with all your heart,
And lean not on your own understanding;
In all your ways acknowledge Him,
And He shall direct your paths (Proverbs 3:5, 6).

Jeanina Bartling

Preface

The creation of this book was not planned. I never set out to write a book. I was simply writing a short Bible study on Luke 8:22–25. As I wrote about the experience of Jesus' disciples on the Sea of Galilee during a windstorm, I realized the lies about God's seeming lack of care we tend to believe when faced with troubles in this world and that cause us to question God when bad things happen.

The topic became intensely fascinating to me. Every time I sat down to write, I had an abundance of ideas to pursue and questions to explore. In my search to better understand God's will for us and why we have to face troubles, this book was born.

As I delved into the subject of who God is in the midst of life's storms, I sensed personally that God wanted me to know and understand Him. In fact, God invites us to discover and investigate Him in the pages of the Bible. That's right, God Himself is inviting us on a journey of discovering who He is:

"And you will seek Me and find Me, when you search for Me with all your heart" (Jeremiah 29:13).

"If you seek Him [inquiring for and of Him and requiring Him as your first and vital necessity] He will let you find Him" (1 Chronicles 28:9, AMP).

"Seek the Lord while He may be found;

> Call on Him [for salvation] while He is near.
> Let the wicked leave (behind) his way
> And the unrighteous man his thoughts;
> And let him return to the LORD,
> And He will have compassion (mercy) on him,
> And to our God,
> For He will abundantly pardon" (Isaiah 55:6, 7, AMP).

"Ask, and it will be given to you; seek, and you will find; knock, and it will be opened to you. For everyone who asks receives, and he who seeks finds, and to him who knocks it will be opened" (Matthew 7:7, 8).

God wants us to investigate Him, discover Him, and seek Him. While there are some aspects of God that are infinitely beyond our comprehension, there are plenty of things that have been revealed to us in His Word, and they are for us to study and accept. "The secret things belong to the LORD our God, but those things which are revealed belong to us and to our children forever, that we may do all the words of this law" (Deuteronomy 29:29).

Our understanding of God is not meant to be based purely on emotionalism or some kind of feel-good belief that has no basis other than it sounds nice or it feels right. Our understanding of God is like building a relationship, and it includes an intellectual and intelligent investigation of who God is. This knowledge comes from going to the Bible, asking questions, and looking for those answers within God's inspired Word. We are invited to search, knock, ask, seek, know, and learn. God invites us to enter into both an emotional experience and an intellectual discovery of Him.

I have faced trial and tribulation. I have asked the same questions about God that many other people have asked, and I have had the same doubts about God during these times as many other people have. I write from a combination of personal experience and deep Bible study on the topic.

When this manuscript was nearly finished, I began to realize the remarkable effect that writing it had on my life. For example, I used to meet bad winter weather with severe contempt and complaints. I know that might sound silly to some people, but to me, it was a big deal. But winter weather, everyday trials, and big troubles began to look different to me. I was surprised to find true acceptance and peace in the storms of life. I began to understand that the writing of this book had drastically changed my own outlook on life and my walk with God. It had been a pivotal point in my life—spiritually, mentally, and emotionally.

Trouble can come from any direction and at any moment. When it hits, it hurts. It can leave us shocked and surprised.

Just before I had applied the finishing touches to the last chapter of the book, trouble came my way. I remember calling my husband on the phone, "Nathan, you better get over here! We have an emergency! Bring lots of towels." We were living in a camper trailer, and it was flooding. The main water line to our camper had frozen (like it usually did) on particularly cold winter nights, but this time the valve to the sewer hose had frozen as well, so no water could exit the camper into the sewer.

On that day, the faucet had been left open in the kitchen sink by accident. I came into the camper after a few hours to find water gushing into the sink. It had filled the gray water tank and caused the bathtub to overflow into the heater vents, filling them with water too. Then the water had begun running out the back end of the camper, soaking the insulation on the underside of the trailer. Any kind of water damage, such as flooding and leaks, is really bad news in a camper. Water can easily get trapped in a camper's walls, ceilings, and flooring; it can quickly rot the cheap plywood that a camper is made of. It seemed we had just destroyed our cozy little home!

I turned off the water and scrambled to sop up the flood with bath towels while my husband scooped the overflowing water from the bathtub and poured it outside. Our home, our little place of refuge and joy, had potentially been destroyed, and I cried at the thought of the loss. But at the same time, I was not worried, enraged, or distraught. I knew that God had a plan and that He would help us. I found myself standing in the middle of a disaster completely at peace. Strangely, I was more excited than ever to see God work on my behalf!

I was so amazed at the peace and acceptance that Jesus had given me in my sudden trial. Everything that I had learned during the writing of this book had clarified my own understanding of how God would work in my life amid trials. I have begun to see more clearly the purpose of the troubles that come my way and who God is in the midst of those problems. My faith has dramatically increased, my relationship with Jesus has been wonderfully enriched, and my outlook on life has drastically changed for the better.

In this book, I'll take a hard, realistic, and raw look at who God is when bad things hit us. I want the truth. If there is assurance to be found, I want it. If there is peace to be grasped, I want it. I want the hard evidence, practical truths, tangible beliefs, and solid conclusions. If you want to understand who God is and where He is in tragedy and affliction, then I encourage you to read and study the following chapters with a willing, open mind. The lessons and discoveries in this book have the potential to change your life for the better. I say this with strong conviction and deep humility that is based on an abiding gratitude to God, without whose help we could accomplish absolutely nothing good.

Introduction

Horatio G. Spafford was a lawyer and businessman living in Chicago. He and his wife, Anna, had four children. In 1871, the Great Chicago Fire destroyed much of their real estate investments.

In 1873, Anna and their four girls traveled to Europe. Horatio had planned to go, but he ended up staying behind to deal with an unforeseen business issue. He intended to join his family a few days later.

Anna and their four girls boarded the ship *Ville du Havre*. While crossing the Atlantic, their ship crashed into an iron-hulled Scottish ship—the *Loch Earn*. Within minutes, the *Ville du Havre* sank, carrying with it 226 passengers. Only eighty-seven people survived. Nine days later, a rescue ship landed in Cardiff, Wales, with the survivors. From there, Anna wired her husband a message that began, "Saved alone[;] what shall I do."

Upon receiving his wife's telegram, Horatio booked passage on the next available ship in order to join his grieving wife. About four days out, the ship's captain called Horatio to his cabin and told him they were passing over the place where his children had drowned. One can only imagine the grief he must have felt. It was at this time that he penned the words to the now-famous hymn:

When peace, like a river, attendeth my way,
When sorrows like sea billows roll;
Whatever my lot, Thou hast taught me to say,

It is well, it is well with my soul.[1]

Anna and Horatio had three more children; one of whom died at the age of four from scarlet fever. Their lives, as are many of ours, were not exempt from pain, tears, and trial. Yet why could Horatio say that whatever his lot, whatever happened, God had taught him to say, "It is well with my soul"? How could peace attend his way, no matter what grief he faced? What gave his grieving heart an anchor in the turbulent storms of his life? What kind of peace calmed the raging waves of sorrow and grief that crashed so powerfully upon his shore? What did God teach him that gave him such confidence, no matter what happened to him or his loved ones?

These are the answers we will seek in the pages ahead.

---

1. Horatio G. Spafford, "It Is Well With My Soul," 1873.

Chapter 1

A Disrupted Journey

Many people gathered around Jesus to hear Him speak by the Sea of Galilee. In fact, so many had come that He waded into the water, climbed into a nearby boat, and continued to teach them from the boat, using it as a platform so that all could hear and see Him.

He taught them many things, speaking in parables and using stories and allegories to help them grasp precious truths. For days, people had followed Him, clamored around Him, and sought Him wherever He went. He had taught, instructed, and encouraged, but now it was time to rest. He said to His disciples, "Let us cross over to the other side of the lake" (Luke 8:22). They sent the people away and entered the boat, setting sail for the other side of the Sea of Galilee.

The Sea of Galilee spread out before them, vast and beautiful. Grebes floated in the shallows, turning their bottoms up as they fed on underwater algae. Armenian gulls flew over the sea; their white bodies glinted in the sunlight. Overhead, little swifts twirled and swooped after insects in the air. The water lapped gently against the sides of the boat. It rocked in peaceful rhythm. Exhausted, Jesus fell asleep in the back of the boat. They sailed along peacefully, and the disciples enjoyed the rest and solitude.

His life of ministry

Jesus' days were busy. Just a few days prior, He had healed a leper. The man, plagued with the contagious malady, had run to Jesus, kneeling before Him. Everyone had recoiled in terror from the man, lest they come in contact with him and be defiled. But Jesus did not run. He had looked at the man with compassion.

"If You are willing, You can make me clean," the leper had cried.

Jesus had reached out and touched him. "I am willing; be cleansed." And immediately the man was healed (Matthew 8:2, 3). There was celebration and joy.

And later in Capernaum, a centurion's servant had been healed of palsy. Then, in Peter's house, Jesus had healed Peter's mother-in-law of a fever. By the end of the day, people had begun bringing the sick and the demon-possessed to Him, and He healed them all (Matthew 8:5–17).

In spite of His miracles and the thoughtful tenderness He showed to everyone, the majority of the religious rulers continued to reject Him as a prophet and the Messiah. They continually sought occasions to argue with and harass Him. They even accused Jesus of being evil (Mark 3:20–30). Nevertheless, Jesus continued to go about the work of His heavenly Father, bringing hope, freedom, and joy to people wherever He went.

The windstorm

Suddenly, the boat in which Jesus and His disciples were traveling jerked from a violent gust of wind, interrupting the peaceful sailing. An explosive squall fell upon the Sea of Galilee. It agitated the water into a fury of battering waves—so much so, that the boat began filling with water. The disciples, buffeted and assailed by the wind and waves, fought to rid the boat of incoming water. The boat reeled and dipped in the angry sea as they scooped up the water with cupped hands, garments, or whatever else they could find. Every time they scooped water out, it seemed that another wave of water poured into the boat. It appeared to fill faster than they could empty it, and every attempt seemed futile. They thought fearfully, *We might actually sink!*

"Awaken Jesus!" one of them yelled.

"Doesn't He care?" another one said.

"Master, Master!" A disciple tapped at Jesus' sleeping form. "We are perishing! Do you not care?"

Jesus awoke. He saw the great storm violently raging around them, waves splattered in His face, and He saw that the disciples were terrified. He saw the water in the boat sloshing and splashing back and forth. He arose. "Peace!" His voice thundered with authority. "Be still!" Immediately, the wind ceased. The great storm that had terrified the disciples had suddenly turned into "a great calm" (Mark 4:39).

Pause. Take in the scene. Listen to the gentle lapping of the water against the boat, with its familiar creaking, and the gentle, rhythmic thump of the ropes on the side of the boat. The wind-torn sails hang quietly, resting. The white-knuckled grip of every man slowly relaxes. Their breaths release.

Jesus fulfilled prophecy by stilling the storm: "He hushed the storm to a gentle whisper, so that the waves of the sea were still" (Psalm 107:29, AMP). "You rule the swelling of the sea; when its waves rise, You still them" (Psalm 89:9, AMP).

Jesus' disciples then stared at Him in awe, saying to one another, "Who then is this, that even the wind and the sea obey Him?" (Mark 4:41, AMP).

What would it have been like to experience a great storm turn abruptly into a great calm, as the Bible describes? The closest I have ever gotten to this type of experience was when I decided one day to get some work done in my garden. As I was outside working, suddenly, the wind rushed upon me. I had seen the storm coming but did not think it would blow in that fast.

The wind pushed and pulled on my clothing. It whipped up the dirt and dried leaves in my winter-worn garden. The pine trees at the edge of the meadow whirled and waved in the unseen air currents. I rushed into the house and shut the door behind me. Holding my breath, I paused in the silence of the house. It was still. It was quiet. It was calm. It was safe.

In the tumultuous experience of Jesus and His disciples on the Sea of Galilee, there are rich lessons for us to dwell upon. Let us consider some of them.

Did Jesus promise smooth sailing across the lake? No.

Jesus never promised His disciples complete calm and safety all the way across the lake. He never said, "Let us cross to the other side of the lake with no problems or struggles or storms." He simply gave them a directive. He pointed them across the lake. He told them of their final destination.

During this storm, the wind-torn and wave-washed disciples turned to Jesus. What did they ask Him? The disciples shouted at Jesus over the raging wind and crashing waves: "Do You not care that we are perishing?" (verse 38).

Was this true? Did Jesus not care whether they perished? Yes, He did care! Oftentimes, when we face difficulties, our first reaction is to ask God, "Do You not care about me? Where are You? Do You not see the trial I am going through?"

Where was Jesus during this storm? He was in the boat *with* them. He was weathering the storm *with* them, but His relationship to the storm was very different from theirs. (We will look more closely at His reaction in later chapters.)

What did Jesus ask them? "Why are you so fearful? How is it that you have no faith?" (verse 40).

Do His questions shock you? They confused me at first because they sounded as though Jesus was being insensitive. I had to spend some time praying and thoughtfully reflecting on what He meant before I came to understand what He was *really* getting at. I concluded that Jesus understood that a situation like they were in would definitely bring out the *feeling* of fear. Fear is a natural human response when we are faced with a seeming life-or-death scenario.

Feeling fearful in a circumstance like the one the disciples faced in the storm is natural. So I think that Jesus' question was aimed at helping them understand why they let fear consume them to the point of thinking that He did not care whether they lived or died. This is the danger of entertaining fear and dwelling in its dark perceptions; it can override the truth. The Bible warns us against this "spirit of fear" in 2 Timothy 1:7: "For God has not given us a spirit of fear, but of power and of love and of a sound mind."

Is the "spirit of fear" from God? No. The spirit of fear locks us into thinking of all the worst possible outcomes. It keeps us up at night, pacing the floor. It paralyzes us. It twists the truth and cripples us. It is this kind of fear that God tells us not to let loose in our minds, because this fear comes from Satan, and he is trying to throw us off balance and keep us from moving forward in faith.

Faith over fear

Look at what Jesus told the disciples before they set sail. Where did He say they were going? "He said to them, 'Let us cross over to the other side of the lake.' And they launched out" (Luke 8:22). So with no apparent worries about their journey, they set sail to the other side of the lake. Notice that Jesus did not say they would "attempt to make it." He said, "We *are* going to the other side." His words were a sure command of confidence.

God has given us every reason to trust Him. If we feel like we lack evidence for that trust in our own lives, the Bible is jam-packed with real-life accounts of His saving the day and making a way where there seemed to be no way. There is far too much evidence throughout the Bible of God's providential intervention in dangerous situations for us to lose faith when we face danger.

The very thing that distorted the disciples' perceptions of Jesus' love and care was the spirit of fear working overtime to corrupt their faith. It is the same spirit of fear that works in our minds to corrupt our faith and distort our perception of God's love and care for us.

Jesus was more reliable and trustworthy than any other person the disciples had ever met. His wisdom and authority extended past anything they had ever heard or seen. He had never let them down or given them a reason to doubt or distrust Him. And on that day, Jesus had told them *ahead of time* exactly where they were going, and they had ample reason based on their past experience with Jesus to completely trust that they would safely end up at their destination—*no matter what might happen in between.* Even though it appeared to the disciples that their boat *could* sink, *they should have known it would not* because Jesus had promised they would surely arrive at their destination.

In the middle of this violent windstorm, they lost sight of God's ability to follow through with His divine plan for their lives. God's Word, His foresight, His vision, and His initiative for them *was like a promise that would prevail no matter how dire their situation or how dangerous their circumstances might have seemed during the journey.* Hence, Jesus' question: "Why do *you* fear? Why do *you* have so little faith? Because what I have promised, that I will surely fulfill."

Before we tumble into lamenting over our wobbly faith, especially in trying circumstances, it is important to understand that we have an enemy seeking to destroy our faith, and his tactics are at work on every level in our lives. "Be sober [well balanced and self-disciplined], be alert and cautious at all times. That enemy of yours, the devil, prowls around like a roaring lion [fiercely hungry], seeking someone to devour" (1 Peter 5:8, AMP).

The devil is not a strange-looking creature with a pitchfork and hooves for feet, but a powerful, beautiful angel fallen from heaven. The Bible explains that "war broke out in heaven" as one of the highest angels became corrupt in his thinking, envious of God, and increasingly selfish (Revelation 12:7). Eventually, "the great dragon was cast out, that serpent of old, called the Devil and Satan, who deceives the whole world; he was cast to the earth, and his angels were cast out with him" (verse 9). Further, the Bible warns us that "Satan himself transforms himself into an angel of light" (2 Corinthians 11:14).

His very first attack on the innocent couple in the Garden of Eden was to introduce a twisted insinuation, a clever deception, and a careful manipulation of the facts that God had laid out to Adam and Eve. It was Satan's plan to instill doubt in God's word and guidance, and that is still one of his highest aims today.

Sometimes God's plan is vivid in our minds, and we launch forth, following His guidance, aiming in the right direction, with every intention of following through to the other side of the lake, so to speak, like Jesus has told us to do. But as we set sail, unexpected trouble comes down upon us, and it greatly disrupts our journey.

Suddenly, our intent to make it to the other side of the lake turns into simply trying to hang on and bail the water from the boat. The struggle consumes our minds. No longer can we see with the eyes of faith the intended destination and the divine plan. And no longer do we trust that God can actually bring us safely into the harbor.

Notice how Satan works on our minds: in the midst of a sudden, stormy trouble, he uses fear and confusion to cause us to doubt God's Word and guidance. Driven by the spirit of fear, doubt starts to overrule our faith.

Oftentimes, our vision of the journey of our lives is a vision of smooth sailing, silent waters, and beautiful sunsets. And when that vision is turned upside down, we tend to doubt God's Word, His provision, His love, and His care for us. Suffering is never on our agenda, so we tend to wonder how it could possibly be part of God's plan for us!

Finding ourselves in a great storm, where it appears that we might perish, does not mean that God does not care about us or love us. It is easy to trust God when the waters are calm, but God wants us to learn to trust Him *in the storm*.

Chapter 2

Plan and Promise

During a severe drought that lasted seven years, God provided for Jacob and his family by strategically placing one of Jacob's sons, Joseph, as a ruler of Egypt, second only to the pharaoh (Genesis 41:37–44; 46:1–6). Jacob, who had been renamed Israel by God (Genesis 35:10), settled and stayed in Egypt. Hundreds of years later, a new Pharaoh arose that did not know anything about the history of Jacob's descendants or about Joseph. Fearful of the Israelites' prosperity and vast numbers, the new Pharaoh enslaved the children of Israel (Exodus 1:8–14).

God had a plan to set His people free. God had chosen an Israelite named Moses to lead His people from the land of Egypt. The problem was that Pharaoh did not want to let the Israelites go. God sent ten plagues across Egypt to convince Pharaoh to let His people go.

Eventually, Pharaoh commanded that they leave, but then he had second thoughts. He sent his army to run them down and bring them back.

But God was guiding the Israelites. During the day, He was a pillar of cloud to provide guidance, and during the night, He was a pillar of fire to provide light (Exodus 13:21, 22). So they traveled day and night. By the time the Egyptians caught up with them, they were already on the edge of the Red Sea.

The Israelites were trapped, caught between a great expanse of water and a great army. We can imagine the spirit of fear growing among the people as, in terror, they began to fully realize the dilemma they were in. They cried, "It would have been better for us to serve the Egyptians than that we should die in the wilderness" (Exodus 14:12). God had preserved, protected, and freed the Israelites from Egyptian slavery, but had He done all that for nothing? Had He brought them to that spot, between the Egyptian army and the Red Sea, to die? These were huge questions in the minds of the Israelites.

Do you hear an echo of the same words Jesus' disciples uttered when they thought they would drown in the stormy sea? "Jesus, do You not care about us?"

Have you ever felt that some battles are just too big to fight? Maybe you have been on the run, only to find yourself trapped between the Red Sea and the enemy whom you've been running from. *Now what? Does God not see me? Does He not understand that I am tired and worn out and trapped?*

Moses shouted to the people, "Fear not!"

Sure, they were in a frightening situation, but Moses did not want the spirit of fear to lead them to doubt God's care for them or His ability to continue to deliver them.

"The Egyptians," Moses said, "whom you see today, you shall see again no more forever. The Lord will fight for you" (verses 13, 14). In other words, God would intervene on their behalf so their enemy would no longer enslave them, harass them, or pursue them. God would destroy their enemy *that* very day!

God instructed Moses to have the Israelites move toward the sea (verse 15). Go where? He told them to keep moving forward. In other words, He told them not to give up. He told them not to think that this was some dreaded end for them, but He still had a plan, as He always does. The same goes for you as well. Don't stop! Keep moving forward in faith! Before you think that it is all over and you might as well throw in the towel, *God is not done!*

Just when all seemed lost, Moses lifted up his arm and stretched his rod over the waters of the Red Sea, following God's direction. When he did, God caused a strong east wind to divide the waters and open a path. On either side of the path was a wall of water. The

Israelites walked through the Red Sea on dry land. *On dry land!* And just like that, God had opened up an unlikely path.

We usually do not see the solutions God sees, and I think it is because we cannot do what He can do. We cannot part the waters of the sea and walk across on dry land, so why would we even think that could be a possibility? God is not bound by the limitations of this physical world. By His word, He created the stars and the moon, the earth, and every living thing. "Ah, Lord God! Behold, You have made the heavens and the earth by Your great power and outstretched arm. There is nothing too hard for You," says Jeremiah the prophet (Jeremiah 32:17). And God says of Himself, "Behold, I am the Lord, the God of all flesh. Is there anything too hard for Me?" (verse 27). *Nothing* is too hard for God. There will never be a problem we face for which He does not already have a totally unthought-of solution. His strength will never fail. His wisdom will never end. His power will never cease. His love will never fade.

God says,

"My thoughts are not your thoughts,
Nor are your ways My ways," says the Lord.
"For as the heavens are higher than the earth,
So are My ways higher than your ways,
And My thoughts than your thoughts" (Isaiah 55:8, 9).

"With God all things are possible" (Matthew 19:26).

It is so important to remember this when we find ourselves hedged in with no obvious ways of escape or solutions to our problems. We can always be assured that God has a way out that we have not even thought of. In fact, He has a thousand ways and a million different solutions that have never even crossed our minds! What is there to fear when God is on our side?

As the Israelites finished crossing through the sea on dry land, the emboldened Egyptians began their pursuit. When the army rushed after the children of Israel, the walls of water began to fall upon them. Soon the entire Egyptian army had drowned in the sea.

No enemy would be allowed to follow the divine path that had been given to the people who had put their trust in God's leading. Today God also promises to save those who put their trust in Him. David records His promise, "And those who know Your name will put their trust in You; for You, Lord, have not forsaken those who seek You" (Psalm 9:10). "Show Your marvelous lovingkindness by Your right hand, O You who save those who trust in You from those who rise up against them" (Psalm 17:7).

As the Israelites watched God save them from the Egyptians, they were amazed! Moses began to praise God in song:

> [God] has triumphed gloriously! . . .
> The Lord is my strength and song,
> And He has become my salvation;
> He is my God, and I will praise Him. . . .
> You in Your mercy have led forth
> The people whom You have redeemed;
> You have guided them in Your strength
> To Your holy habitation (Exodus 15:1, 2, 13).

So not only is God perfectly able to solve *every one* of our problems, but He redeems us, He leads us in mercy, and He guides us in His strength. We could not be in better hands!

Chapter 3

Peace and Trouble

After the crossing of the Red Sea, the Israelites continued their journey to the Promised Land. After a time, they began to notice that their food supply was decreasing rapidly and their flocks were diminishing. It would not be long before they would have nothing to eat. They mulled over what could happen. They and their children *could* starve to death! The longer they dwelt upon what *could* happen, the less they remembered the God who had redeemed them from death and destruction just a short while ago.

Though they had *not yet* experienced hunger, they began to be greatly troubled, and they began to complain.

"Then the whole congregation of the children of Israel complained against Moses and Aaron in the wilderness. And the children of Israel said to them, 'Oh, that we had died by the hand of the Lord in the land of Egypt, when we sat by the pots of meat and when we ate bread to the full! For you have brought us out into this wilderness to kill this whole assembly with hunger' " (Exodus 16:2, 3).

Moses was simply following God's plan, so the accusations, even though apparently aimed at Moses and Aaron, were actually targeted at God. What did they accuse God of? Of leading them into the wilderness to die of hunger. Was it reasonable to think that God would lead them through the Red Sea only to have them starve to death in the wilderness? Did you notice that the distrust the Israelites expressed when facing hunger was the very same kind of distrust they had demonstrated when they found themselves trapped by the

Red Sea? And it was the same distrust they had shown when they had run out of water three days after crossing the Red Sea (Exodus 15:23–27)—a water problem that God had miraculously solved. The familiar question was asked once again: Does God not see this problem? Does He not care about us?

Doubt is a serious, recurring problem for God's people when they face difficulties.

To be clear: hardship and trial were not new experiences for the Israelites. Pharaoh had made their lives very difficult (Exodus 1:13, 14). Although their lives in Egypt had been extremely hard, they had been well fed. But now, as their food decreased, they feared starvation in this desolate, barren wilderness. As they dwelt upon what they *thought might happen*, they began to admit that they would rather have stayed in bondage and in an unhealthy and oppressive lifestyle for the sake of a few comforts they had apparently never lacked, rather than be liberated by God and learn to trust His provision. This admission reveals how great the human desire is for comfort and supposed certainty at any cost.

It is hard to believe that any of us would choose slavery over freedom, but we see it here! The Israelites were real people, like you and me, and though they lived many centuries ago, they reflect human nature in a way that is also real to us. The Bible encourages us to emulate the heroic actions of the faith of God's people who lived long ago. Their ancient lives also teach us to avoid the pitfalls of distrust and the unsettling of fear as we make life choices today.

Satan does not want his slaves to go free, so he will try to lure those who have received Christ's freedom back into slavery any way he can. Part of his plan is to make us *think* that God's way of life is too barren, too uncertain, and too uncomfortable. Thus, Satan tempts us to believe we would be better off if we just backslid into his grasp again. There is always something that Satan will bring out about that old way of life to make it attractive to us.

Hungering for a stronger faith

As we choose to follow Jesus, every journey with Him includes a series of tests and trials that God allows to happen in our lives. They are opportunities to learn to trust Him more. As our experiences with Him grow, our faith and trust in Him deepens. We need to be aware that Satan also uses those same tests and trials to discourage us. Our enemy speaks deceptively to us: "If God really cared about you, He would keep you from experiencing the troubles you are going through right now, wouldn't He?"

Just as Jesus never promised His disciples smooth sailing across the Sea of Galilee, He does not promise us, His modern-day disciples, smooth sailing either. There are going to be struggles. There are going to be troubles.

In John 16:32, Jesus warned His disciples that a hard time was soon coming upon them: "Indeed the hour is coming, yes, has now come, that you will be scattered, each to his own, and will leave Me alone. And yet I am not alone, because the Father is with Me." In fact, this upcoming trial that Jesus was talking about would be so intense that it would scatter the disciples. He wanted to warn them ahead of time so that they could choose to be grounded in faith and trust when He was crucified (John 14:29).

Because God knows about our troubles ahead of time, He can also provide a way to endure them. What a beautiful thought! We read in 1 Corinthians 10:13 that "no temptation has overtaken you except such as is common to man; but God is faithful, who will not allow you to be tempted beyond what you are able, but with the temptation will also make the way of escape, that you may be able to bear it."

Temptations come at all times and in all shapes and sizes, but they hit really hard when we are already in a difficult situation. We may think of temptations primarily in terms of desires, but in tough times, there is an even greater temptation, and that is to give up and walk away from God.

There is a strong temptation to believe the enemy's distorted lies about God when we are assailed by trouble and uncertainty. These lies try to convince us that God does not care about us or love us enough to take care of us. But the Bible does not say that He will always remove the temptation when we ask, but it does say that He provides a way of escape so that we can endure it. This endurance is found in trusting God to strengthen us to resist the enemy's lies and avoid falling into doubt and fear.

Check out this insight from Jesus in John 16:33. He says, "These things I have spoken to you, that in Me you may have peace. In the world you will have tribulation; but be of good cheer, I have overcome the world." After telling His disciples they would soon go through a extremely difficult time, what did Jesus say they would have in this world? *Tribulation!*

Tribulation means "trouble." Jesus wanted them to know, ahead of time, that they would not be exempt from the troubles in this world. Peter affirms this: "Be sober, be vigilant; because your adversary the devil walks about like a roaring lion, seeking whom he may devour" (1 Peter 5:8).

We have an enemy who is always seeking to disrupt our lives and tempt us to surrender to him. It is very clear that while we live in this world, we, both Christians and non-Christians, will have trouble.

Take a moment to think about the following: non-Christians die, and so do Christians. Non-Christians get into car accidents, and so do Christians. Non-Christians get diseases and cancer, and so do Christians. Non-Christians lose their jobs, and so do Christians. Bad things happen to non-Christians, and bad things happen to Christians. Everyone suffers and everyone struggles—both Christians and non-Christians. "OK," you might ask, "if bad things happen to both Christians and non-Christians, then why choose to be a Christian? What is the difference?" Let us continue to explore the answers to these question.

Peace in the storm

Let us take another look at John 16:33: "These things I have spoken to you, that in Me you may have peace. In the world you will have tribulation; but be of good cheer, I have overcome the world."

Jesus told the disciples that in Him, they can have what? Peace. Even though they had—and we will have—trouble, they could know that in God there is peace. Notice that the peace is *in Him*, by abiding in Him, by being connected with Him, and by trusting Him. We can soak that peace deep into our souls by seeking Him and spending time with Him in prayer, praise, and study of His Word. *When troubles come, our constant connection with Him will impart a deep, abiding peace in Him.*

In John 14:27, Jesus said, "Peace I leave with you; My [perfect] peace I give to you; not as the world gives do I give to you. Do not let your heart be troubled, nor let it be afraid. [Let My perfect peace calm you in every circumstance and give you courage and strength for every challenge]" (AMP).

Is the peace that Jesus gives us like the world's version of peace? No! The only kind of peace the world gives is fleeting and short lived. It is sketchy and unreliable; it is something you have to conjure up from nothing. The peace that Jesus gives is a special kind of peace.

Why is the peace that Jesus gives different? We read in Philippians 4:7: "And the peace of God [that peace which reassures the heart, that peace] which transcends all understanding, [that peace which] stands guard over your hearts and your minds in Christ Jesus [is yours]" (AMP).

Jesus' peace goes beyond all human understanding and anchors us to Him in the storm. When our adverse circumstances give rise to uncertainty (like the Israelites' food shortage), trusting that Jesus loves us, cares about us, and has a plan for us, gives us a peace that transcends the current problems. When circumstances give rise to undeniable fear (like the disciples' experience of being out at sea in a little wooden boat in a great storm), placing our trusting eyes upon Jesus will soothe our fears and give us a peace that transcends the current troubles.

When in a little boat in a big storm, the common thing to do is frantically scramble for ways to survive, but that takes us only so far before we run out of options and ideas. We may feel like the only alternative left is accepting that we are simply at the mercy of the wind and the waves and drowning may be our ultimate fate. This obviously thrusts us into all sorts of frantic, panic-stricken thoughts, words, and actions.

But the Bible tells us that the peace that Jesus gives us surpasses all rational, logical human reasoning, and His peace will guide our response to the troubles we face. Take a moment to consider Jesus. He was in the *same* boat and in the *same* storm as His disciples, but His reaction to the storm was very different.

Obviously, Jesus was tired—very tired. That is why He fell asleep. But the fact that He remained asleep while the storm raged around Him is absolutely mind-boggling. Just think for a moment about the sound of the howling, tugging winds and the spray of water upon Him, the lurching of the boat up and down on the waves. Any ordinary person would be terrified under those circumstances!

Strangely, Jesus was unmoved, untouched, and apparently unconcerned by the storm that seemed so threatening to the disciples. But Jesus had peace because He knew His Father had a plan. He was confident in His Father's will and Word, His presence and His promises. He had a peace that was beyond comprehension—a peace the storm could not touch or steal away. There is something very special about what God's peace can do for us, which is exemplified so beautifully in the life of Jesus.

Consider Philippians 4:7 again: "And the peace of God, which surpasses all understanding, will guard your hearts and minds through Christ Jesus."

Notice that this peace shall *keep* our hearts and minds through Christ Jesus. We do not experience God's peace because He takes away the storm, but His peace has the power to keep or "guard" our hearts and minds in the midst of the raging storm. How important is this? What does it mean?

When we encounter threatening circumstances, the human mind can invent all sorts of crazy, fear-induced ideas and actions. All sorts of illogical thoughts and ideas can come racing to our minds and prompt a whole array of foolish reactions that worsen the situation.

We hear of people trampling and killing each other in their frantic attempts to escape something they thought could hurt or kill them. Given the right conditions, people, taken by fear, may jump off a cliff to avoid something they thought could kill them. Fear of starvation induced the Israelites to want to rush back to a life of slavery! Fear like this doesn't make sense. Fear like this can blind people to reality and control their actions. Fear like this can make people do all sorts of irrational things—horrible things—that they would not have done if they had been thinking straight. And the frightening fact is that, sometimes, we are those people!

Here is where God's peace comes in. It changes us and guards us from going off the deep end and acting irrationally. His peace calms us and secures us to Him. We recognize that we are under His wings and in His hands (Psalm 17:8; John 10:28–30). He is our Anchor and our Hope (Hebrews 6:19). His peace keeps our minds focused and our thoughts realistic. Our emotions find solid ground in Him, and we are able to move forward, calmly and trustfully.

To the rest of the world, this calmness, this level-headedness under stress, seems strange, confusing, and even out of reach. But if we trust in Jesus, God's peace lifts us up and into His perspective, assuring us that He has a plan and a purpose for each of us and that we can trust Him to fulfill that plan, no matter what happens along the way. His peace glues us to Him and anchors us to the truth of His Word and His promises.

We know that troubles come upon Christians and non-Christians, but Christians can have divine peace in the storm.

Chapter 4

Provision and Promise

In the last chapter, we read about the Israelites' fear of future starvation. Now we'll look at God's solution for their future problem.

> And the LORD spoke to Moses, saying, "I have heard the complaints of the children of Israel. Speak to them, saying, 'At twilight you shall eat meat, and in the morning you shall be filled with bread. And you shall know that I am the LORD your God.'"
>
> So it was that quail came up at evening and covered the camp, and in the morning the dew lay all around the camp. And when the layer of dew lifted, there, on the surface of the wilderness, was a small round substance, as fine as frost on the ground. So when the children of Israel saw it, they said to one another, "What is it?" For they did not know what it was.
>
> And Moses said to them, "This is the bread which the LORD has given you to eat" (Exodus 16:11–15).

When the Israelites saw this white substance covering the ground, they called it *manna*, which means "What is it?" They had never seen it before.

Instructed by God, Moses told them to "gather it according to each one's need, one omer for each person, according to the number of persons; let every man take for those who are in his tent" (verse 16). (An *omer* is a biblical unit of measure for dry grain that is equivalent to approximately two quarts.) They were to collect only what they needed per person for that day, and it would be sufficient to meet their nutritional needs.

So they gathered what they needed, and Moses warned them, "Let no one leave any of it till morning" (verse 19). Nevertheless, some people did not trust Moses' instruction. They worried that the manna (bread) might not fall again, so they saved some of their manna for later, and the next morning it had spoiled.

Consider Matthew 6:31–33, where we read Jesus' counsel: "Therefore do not worry, saying, 'What shall we eat?' or 'What shall we drink?' or 'What shall we wear?' For after all these things the Gentiles seek. For your heavenly Father knows that you need all these things. But seek first the kingdom of God and His righteousness, and all these things shall be added to you."

Does God know our needs? There are many storms and trials that are accompanied by a lack of basic needs, such as food and shelter. Oftentimes, it seems like when things go wrong, they really go wrong. It is always the enemy's intent to use the lack of essentials to instill doubt about God's personal care for us.

But the Bible says that God knows our needs before we even ask (see verse 8). It is reassuring to realize that God already knows what our basic needs are. Philippians 4:6 tells us: "Do not be anxious or worried about anything, but in everything [every circumstance and situation] by prayer and petition with thanksgiving, continue to make your [specific] requests known to God" (AMP).

Even though God knows our needs, it is important to bring them to Him in prayer, asking respectfully and claiming His promises. But here is the deal: Having done that, we do not need to agonize and fret about them anymore! Once we have placed them in God's hands, we can know that He is working on it. As God provided daily bread from heaven to feed His people, His instruction was, "Trust Me." Every day the Israelites were to gather the exact amount of manna needed per person, nothing more and nothing less. Their daily lesson was to be that God will provide, so they did not need to worry about tomorrow. *They were to trust in God's provision before*

He provided it. That is faith. Or as the author of Hebrews describes it, "Faith is the substance of things hoped for, the evidence of things not seen" (Hebrews 11:1).

On the sixth day of the week, the Israelites were given special instructions to gather twice as much manna—two omers per person. Moses explained, "This is what the Lord has said: 'Tomorrow is a Sabbath rest, a holy Sabbath to the Lord. Bake what you will bake today, and boil what you will boil; and lay up for yourselves all that remains, to be kept until morning' " (Exodus 16:23).

Here again is a lesson of trust. For five days, they were to gather only what they needed per person for that day. Anything saved would rot. But on the sixth day, they were to gather twice as much manna per person and save it for the next day. How would they know that it would not rot like it did on the other five days? They could know that God had assured them that it would be preserved for that special Sabbath day. "So they laid it up till morning, as Moses commanded; and it did not stink, nor were there any worms in it. Then Moses said, 'Eat that today, for today is a Sabbath to the Lord; today you will not find it in the field. Six days you shall gather it, but on the seventh day, the Sabbath, there will be none' " (verses 24–26). It is was a miracle!

Resting and trusting in God

Here is a special blessing to be noticed: The seventh day was the Sabbath, which is a day of rest. It was God's original design, instituted at the creation of the world, that we should have a special blessing of rest on the seventh day of the week. God knew that we would need it! And on this special, holy day, everyone has the privilege of resting from a busy week of work. Referring back to the Creation story, we read, "Thus the heavens and the earth, and all the host of them, were finished. And on the seventh day God ended His work which He had done, and He rested on the seventh day from all His work which He had done. Then God blessed the seventh day and sanctified it, because in it He rested from all His work which God had created and made" (Genesis 2:1–3).

The sixth day, Friday, is described in the Bible as the "Preparation" day before the Sabbath (John 19:31; Mark 15:42; Luke 23:54; Matthew 27:62). On this day, we can prepare for the Sabbath, as the Israelites did, by preparing our food ahead of time and preparing our hearts to rest in God.

At the end of the preparation day, we have God's consent to walk away from unfinished projects and rest in the presence of the Almighty God. We do not need to worry about what has been left undone at the end of the week. On the Sabbath day, we can truly rest—from work, from concerns, from deadlines, from pressures, and from demands. We can know that as we rest, God will refresh us, strengthen us, and encourage us for another week's duties and obligations.

Just like God provided extra bread from heaven to last through the resting hours of the Sabbath, He will make sure our provisions are given and our needs are met while we peacefully rest in Him.

While we may think that the manna God provided seems boring, the Bible tells us that "it tasted like flat pastry (wafers) made with honey" (Exodus 16:31, AMP). That sounds amazing to me! God knows that most of us have a sweet tooth. I would not mind eating something like pastry and honey every morning! In any case, we can be assured that it was versatile and that it tasted wonderful. Why? Because God cares about the details we delight in. Just look at the vast array of foods He has provided all over the world. There are all sorts of varieties with different textures, colors, and tastes. We can know that God cares about us and has something planned for us that is not only sufficient but also is wonderful and exciting in so many different ways.

The abundant life

God promises us an abundant life, even in the wilderness. Speaking about our basic needs—what we shall eat, drink, or wear—Jesus says, "Seek first the kingdom of God and His righteousness, and all these things shall be added to you" (Matthew 6:33). Synonymous with that verse is Psalm 37:4: "Delight yourself also in the LORD, and He shall give you the desires of your heart."

When my husband and I got married, we had one vehicle—a 1991 Ford Ranger. Through those first years, we drove that thing all over the place, down highways, up dusty roads, over mountains on rocky trails, and to work and back. By the end of a few years, that truck had seen it all, and it was showing signs of dying. So the time had come to retire it for something new.

We began the search for a new car. We took the need to God in prayer, knowing that He already knew what we needed, but we asked anyway and hoped He would give us the desires of our heart—a car with a sunroof, electric windows and locks, and an automatic transmission (we wanted a break after several years of driving a stick shift). In addition, we wanted the color of the car to be black and preferred a car less than ten years old with really low mileage and all of those features for an affordable price!

It still amazes us today, as we look back on our list of desires, how God took us to the right person selling the exact car we wanted (with *everything* on our list) at a very affordable price. There have been so many times in our lives when we have visibly and tangibly seen the mighty hand of God providing for us in all the little ways we needed and even desired. Sometimes we had to wait for His timing and blessing; we were empty handed for a while before receiving the reward of our faith. Sometimes He gave us just enough; nothing more and nothing less. Sometimes He gave us way beyond what we asked for, because He loves us—God is good—yes, all the time! David testifies,

> Oh, how great is Your goodness,
> Which You have laid up for those who fear You,
> Which You have prepared for those who trust in You
> In the presence of the sons of men! (Psalm 31:19).

Delighting in God

We all want the desires of our heart fulfilled. Sometimes those desires are out of harmony with what God knows is best for us. That is why Matthew 6:33 says, "Seek first the kingdom of God and His righteousness," and Psalm 37:4 says, "Delight yourself also in the LORD." But what does it mean to seek God first and to delight in Him?

Delight is a word that expresses taking joy in something or someone. As we seek to know God and appreciate who He is in splendor, strength, majesty, power, grace, justice, mercy, love, and forgiveness—all the aspects of His personality and His character—then we are truly delighting in Him.

God wants us to discover Him. He invites us, saying, "And you will seek Me and find Me, when you search for Me with all your heart" (Jeremiah 29:13).

God wants us to study Him. He wants us to get to know and comprehend Him as best we can.

Thus says the LORD:

> "Let not the wise man glory in his wisdom,
> Let not the mighty man glory in his might,
> Nor let the rich man glory in his riches;
> But let him who glories glory in this,
> That he understands and knows Me,
> That I am the LORD, exercising lovingkindness, judgment, and righteousness in the earth.
> For in these I delight," says the LORD (Jeremiah 9:23, 24).

In the writing of this book, I spent countless hours investigating God by studying His Word and getting to know Him as my Lord and King. Discovering who God is in the midst of life's storms was an amazing journey.

The apostle Paul, who had once enjoyed being part of the top tiers of his culture and society, considered all that he once had—fame, authority, and knowledge—simply worthless compared to what he had discovered in Jesus Christ (Philippians 3:1–12). He was willing to walk away from all he had previously considered as best into learning all about Jesus and walking with Him, which was truly, without a doubt, everything he needed and more. He had concluded that knowing Jesus was the best thing that had ever happened to him. No doubt Paul echoed David's cry: "Oh, taste and see that the LORD is good; blessed is the man who trusts in Him!" (Psalm 34:8). This very personal and intimate study into discovering who Jesus is has been the most invigorating, life-changing experience of my life. And God invites everyone to experience the same.

There are times God leads us through the barren wilderness as a necessary part of our journey, just like it was for the Israelites. Through our troubles in this world—the ones we are now in and the ones on the horizon—God is saying to us, "Trust Me." Truly, "we know [with great confidence] that God [who is deeply concerned about us] causes all things to work together [as a plan] for good for those who love God, to those who are called according to His plan and purpose" (Romans 8:28, AMP).

Through the entire forty years of living in the wilderness, God's people were never forsaken. He continued to guide them and provide for them. Exodus 16:35 records that God fed His people bread from heaven for forty years. Not only that, we also know that God took care of all of their basic needs. "And I have led you forty years in the wilderness. Your clothes have not worn out on you, and your sandals have not worn out on your feet" (Deuteronomy 29:5). Think about that!

The experience of the Israelites' time in the wilderness has valuable lessons for us today. Their wilderness journey reminds us that we can trust God's providence and His care for us regardless of the circumstances we are in or the places we are traveling through. In truth, "You will show me the path of life; in Your presence is fullness of joy; at Your right hand are pleasures forevermore" (Psalm 16:11).

Chapter 5

Bread From Heaven

In the last chapter, we saw how God provided for the physical needs of His people by giving them bread from heaven. The Israelites did not understand it at the time, but God was revealing a picture of Himself to them and to everyone who thirsts for hope and healing.

Taking this picture of provision and promise, Jesus related the Israelites' bread from heaven to Himself. Here He used a historical experience as a symbol of His current mission. As a large crowd had gathered to hear Jesus speak, He began to teach. Among the crowd were the religious rulers, who were suspicious of Jesus' growing fame and influence on the people. They wanted Jesus to prove that He was sent from God. They were looking for a miraculous sign before they would believe, saying, "Our fathers ate the manna in the desert; as it is written, 'He gave them bread from heaven to eat' " (John 6:31). For them, that was a miracle that they could believe in—a visible manifestation of God's providence and blessing. They wanted Jesus to give them a sign that God's same providence and blessing were in Him before they would believe that He was sent from God.

Jesus agreed with the religious leaders that God had fed the Israelites in the wilderness and that it was a sign of God's favor, but now, God wanted to give them the "true Bread" from heaven—a Bread that gives life to the world. Jesus warned them, "Do not labor for the food which perishes, but for the food which endures to everlasting life, which the Son of Man will give you, because God the Father has set His seal on Him" (verse 27).

God's seal is a manifestation of His character in a person's life—godly thinking, talking, and behavior—basically how an individual worships and serves God in all he or she does and in every circumstance of his or her life.

Every aspect of Jesus' life, down to the smallest detail, revealed God's seal upon Him. Jesus was the spiritual revelation of the Father's character. The Father's providence and blessing were clearly evident in Jesus' life, from His miraculous healings to His transformative teachings. These should have been sufficient evidence for the Jewish leaders to believe in Jesus.

Jesus told the hungry crowd, "I am the bread of life. He who comes to Me shall never hunger, and he who believes in Me shall never thirst. . . . For I have come down from heaven, not to do My own will, but the will of Him who sent Me" (verses 35, 38).

The bread that the Israelites ate in the desert did not give them eternal life. It provided only temporal sustenance, but it symbolically pointed to the time when God would send His Son to give up His life for the world so that "whoever believes in Him should not perish but have everlasting life" (John 3:16).

The manna in the wilderness revealed that God was interested in providing for our temporary needs—food and water, clothing and shelter. But His deepest interest, His real desire, is that we will seek spiritual manna and eternal life, given only through the real Bread from heaven: Jesus Christ.

If you hunger and thirst for spiritual enlightenment, spiritual food, then God has provided spiritual nourishment for your soul through His Son, Jesus. He described it this way: "It is the Spirit who gives life; the flesh conveys no benefit [it is of no account]. The words I have spoken to you are spirit and life [providing eternal life]" (John 6:63, AMP). In other words, seeking after physical things in this world will not bring about spiritual health or enlightenment. Only by seeking Jesus, reading and studying His words, and believing in Him will we be spiritually nourished. This is important to remember when we are going through difficult times that test our faith in God. With every temporal need that God fulfills, His real intent is to draw us to Him for spiritual food. And that is the case as well when we find ourselves at a loss or experience a physical want or disaster. *It is spiritual nourishment from Jesus that provides strength and inspires faith when we are in the wilderness, walking through test and trial.*

Our greatest need

When we are seeking to have our needs filled, God is *the answer*. And this is not just because He is the only One who can fill those needs according to His divine plan but also because of everything that we really need in this world: Jesus is our *greatest need*. Let me use an analogy to explain.

Have you ever lost your car keys right when you needed them the most? What is the first thing you do? (You know where I am going, right?) The next few minutes entail a wild scramble of looking through pants pockets, coat pockets, drawers, tabletops, countertops, purses, backpacks, whatever! It never ceases to amaze me how perplexing the loss of car keys can be, because without keys, we are not going anywhere!

When we are stuck in difficult times, the first thing God wants us to do is focus our energies on Him—who He is and how we can be closer members of His family. He yearns for us to make prayer our first impulse. He wants us to run to His Word for wisdom. He wants us to seek Him with all of our hearts and strength because He is the Possessor of everything we need (see Deuteronomy 4:29). The truth is, we are not going to arrive at any good destination without Him. He is our ticket out of *every* dilemma. He is the key that unlocks the door and turns on the engine to our hearts so that we can move forward in faith.

When life goes awry, our outlook often follows the same path. This is where the enemy really starts working to distort and sour our taste for spiritual things. When bad things happen in our lives, the devil wants us to spiral downward, losing our identity and purpose. Our adversary wants us to think that God has abandoned us and that He does not really care about us.

That is why Jesus tells us to seek Him *first* and stay centered on Him, as it says in Isaiah 26:3: "You will keep in perfect and constant peace the one whose mind is steadfast [that is, committed and focused on You—in both inclination and character], because he trusts and takes refuge in You [with hope and confident expectation]" (AMP).

If we lose sight of Jesus, we lose sight of our identity. That's right, we are the sons and daughters of God (2 Corinthians 6:18), redeemed by His blood—precious and valuable in His sight (Ephesians 1:7; Titus 3:4–7); we belong to Him (Isaiah 43:1); and in Him, all of our needs are met (Philippians 4:19). If the enemy can get us to look at everything except Jesus, we will forget who we are and to whom we belong: we belong to Jesus, and we are part of His family. Just read the following list recorded in Ephesians 1:

- He chose us and has a special plan for us (verse 4).
- He planned for us to be adopted as His children (verse 5).
- He freely gave us grace and favor (verse 6).
- He redeemed and forgave us (verses 7, 8).
- He gave us an eternal inheritance (verse 11).
- He gave us the Holy Spirit as His special indwelling presence (verses 13, 14).

Paul, who wrote this beautiful letter to the Ephesians (and it applies just as much to us today), goes on, praying that

> the God of our Lord Jesus Christ, the Father of glory, may grant you a spirit of wisdom and of revelation [that gives you a deep and personal and intimate insight] into the true knowledge of Him [for we know the Father through the Son]. And [I pray] that the eyes of your heart [the very center and core of your being] may be enlightened [flooded with light by the Holy Spirit], so that you will know and cherish the hope [the divine guarantee, the confident expectation] to which He has called you, the riches of His glorious inheritance in the saints (God's people), and [so that you will begin to know] what the

immeasurable and unlimited and surpassing greatness of His [active, spiritual] power is in us who believe. These are in accordance with the working of His mighty strength (verses 17–19, AMP).

It is amazing that the God who created the universe and all that is in it, would be so intimately involved in all the details of our lives. He who told the sun where to shine and put the planets in their orbits has lavished His love and grace upon us so we can be redeemed from the darkness of sin that has enveloped this world and constantly wreaks havoc in our lives.

As a believer grasps and accepts this joyful new identity in Jesus, he or she is encouraged, by the teachings of Jesus Himself, to be baptized. This baptism is symbolic of a new birth and adoption into the family of God. It symbolizes dying to the old, sin-filled, and sin-controlled way of life and being resurrected into new life, living in the power of the Holy Spirit. As my favorite Bible verse says, "I have been crucified with Christ; it is no longer I who live, but Christ lives in me; and the life which I now live in the flesh I live by faith in the Son of God, who loved me and gave Himself for me" (Galatians 2:20). Also speaking of baptism, Colossians 3:1, 2 tells us, "If then you were raised with Christ, seek those things which are above, where Christ is, sitting at the right hand of God. Set your mind on things above, not on things on the earth."

When we choose to follow Christ, our lives become witnesses to His faithfulness. Truly, "for the Lord God is a sun and shield; the Lord bestows grace and favor and honor; no good thing will He withhold from those who walk uprightly" (Psalm 84:11, AMP).

What about tomorrow? God will provide for each day exactly what we need. Yet I have to ask the question: Is that always true? Tomorrow we could find ourselves without jobs or homes. Our moms could die, our spouses could leave us, our best friends could betray us, or we could be injured in an accident.

What about the times when we find ourselves at a loss, grieving the passing of a loved one, or standing in the midst of disaster? What then? Where is God's favor and blessing when bad things happen? Where are the good things He promised?

How is a person who just lost everything supposed to believe that God provides everything when we need it? If God provides for our needs, isn't it true that we wouldn't have any unmet needs?

Even though there will be times when we do not have everything we want, we can be assured that we will always have the good things God has promised. Here is a short list of what God has promised us:

- His peace that surpasses understanding (Philippians 4:7; John 14:27)
- His strength when we are weak (2 Corinthians 12:9, 10)
- His love that knows no end (Romans 5:6–11; 1 John 3:1)
- His mercy every morning (Lamentations 3:22–26)
- His grace and forgiveness for our failings (Ephesians 1:7, 8; 1 John 2:1, 2)
- His Holy Spirit, the Helper, who is always with us (John 15:26; Matthew 28:19, 20)
- His wisdom and spiritual enlightenment (Ephesians 1:17, 18)
- His gift of eternal life and an inheritance (Ephesians 1:18, 19)
- His gift of the resurrection from the dead (John 5:28, 29; 11:25)

These are the good things that have been promised to those who seek God and trust Him. We can always know that we will have these things, *no matter what*! We were not promised smooth sailing with no loss or sorrow. Jesus warned us that we would experience trouble in this world, but the good things Jesus promised (in the list above) will get us through the tough times and will provide everything we need during the discouraging times.

When we find ourselves in the wilderness, in test and trial, in storm and trouble, in grief and sorrow, and in pain and disaster, God often sends people our way to help with food, shelter, and other basic needs. But it is in these times that we need to seek Jesus Himself more than anything else, for our eternal deliverance depends on His *spiritual* provisions. We need to set our focus and affections on God and the things of God and not allow our earthly troubles to cause us to forget who we are in Christ Jesus.

When we find ourselves in hard times, our eyes need to be on the only One who can set us in "heavenly places" (Ephesians 2:4–9) and raise us up in the "last day" (John 6:40).

Chapter 6

The God Who Sees Us

When an onslaught of trouble comes at us fast and furious, it just doesn't seem fair, and we want to know why. We want to know every detail and have a full report! It is OK to ask God why the trial is happening, but please know that He does not always give us a complete answer.

Remember Isaiah 55:8, 9?

"My thoughts are not your thoughts,
Nor are your ways My ways," says the Lord.
"For as the heavens are higher than the earth,
So are My ways higher than your ways,
And My thoughts than your thoughts."

God's thoughts and ways are higher than ours. We may not be able to comprehend the complexities of God's work in our lives and in the lives of those around us. So, instead of telling us why, He often points us to Himself and says, "Just trust Me."

Our Creator God, Jesus, became one of us (Philippians 2:5–8). He came down to our world, walked among us, lived with us, and experienced the hardships, struggles, and weaknesses that we, as humans living in a sinful world, have to experience. Because of this, we can trust that He understands what we are going through, since He went through it too.

After Jesus' resurrection, He became our High Priest. In this position, He is the Intercessor between the Father and us. In other words, Jesus stands in our place before the Father, declaring that, because of His sinless life, willing death, and victorious resurrection on our behalf, we are entitled to receive all of Heaven's benefits.

"Inasmuch then as we [believers] have a great High Priest who has [already ascended and] passed through the heavens, Jesus the Son of God, let us hold fast our confession [of faith and cling tenaciously to our absolute trust in Him as Savior]. For we do not have a High Priest who is unable to sympathize and understand our weaknesses and temptations, but One who has been tempted [knowing exactly how it feels to be human] in every respect as we are, yet without [committing any] sin" (Hebrews 4:14, 15, AMP).

What a blessing to know that our Savior and God intimately knows and understands us and our human experience because He dwelt among us and lived as one of us. Thus, we can trust Him with unconditional peace and assurance.

"Therefore," Hebrews 4 continues, "let us [with privilege] approach the throne of grace [that is, the throne of God's gracious favor] with confidence and without fear, so that we may receive mercy [for our failures] and find [His amazing] grace to help in time of need [an appropriate blessing, coming just at the right moment]" (verse 16, AMP).

Where does the Bible tell us to run when we are in need? To the throne of grace. Running to the throne of grace implies having confidence that when we run there we will obtain grace. What is grace? And how does grace help us in our time of need?

Grace is the free and unmerited favor of God. So when we come to the throne of grace, looking for help, we can know right away that God is on our side and that we can count on His support.

Even though we do not understand exactly what Jesus is doing or how He is working, we can know that He *is* working on our behalf. What is so amazing is that we do not have to try to convince Him or beg Him to help us, nor do we have to somehow earn His favor. We do not have to perform rituals, ceremonies, or contrived methods of appeasement. His grace assures us that He is eager to help us—*free of charge*. There is no merit needed here; all we have to do is come, acknowledging our need! All we have to do is humbly ask.

The Bible tells us to "come *boldly* to the throne" (verse 16; emphasis added). Yes, you! Yes, me! Each one of us is personally invited to come to God's throne. We can come boldly because Jesus opened the door of heaven to us. This personal invitation means that no "holy" man or women, priest, teacher, theologian, professor, pastor, or religious leader needs to intercede on our behalf. We already have a High Priest, an Intercessor, and an Advocate when we come to the throne—His name is Jesus. "If anyone sins, we have an Advocate with the Father, Jesus Christ the righteous. And He Himself is the propitiation for our sins, and not for ours only but also for the whole world" (1 John 2:1, 2).

Propitiation means atonement for our sins. Jesus has paid the price, the consequences, for our sins. It is our sin that separates us from God, but Jesus has bridged the separation between God and us. The good news is that each one of us can boldly come to the throne of grace!

Mercy in time of need

The author of Hebrews encourages believers to "come boldly to the throne of grace, that we may obtain mercy and find grace to help in time of need" (Hebrews 4:16). God's mercy is never in short supply, but sometimes the only mercy we are seeking is for God to take the trouble we are in right out of our lives. God does sometimes take some troubles and trials right out of our paths. But strange as it may sound, taking every trial from us, especially right away, is not always God's will. So His mercy is to be seen and understood in the context of suffering and patience.

> The LORD is gracious and full of compassion,
> Slow to anger and great in mercy.
> The LORD is good to all,
> And His tender mercies are over all His works (Psalm 145:8, 9).

God's mercy is over how much of His work? *All* of His work! In other words, there is not a work He does that is not full of His mercy and compassion. So, whatever trouble He allows to come our way, He has already approved it with His mercy.

In one of his darkest times, the prophet Jeremiah wrote some of the most sorrowful verses in the Bible. In Lamentations 3, he wrote as if hope had been nearly lost. He spoke of pain and hardship as being an overwhelming torrent against him. Yet, in thinking about these tragedies that had humbled him, he chose to call to mind specific attributes of God's character that filled him with hope.

> This I recall to my mind,
> Therefore I have hope.
> Through the Lord's mercies we are not consumed,
> Because His compassions fail not.
> They are new every morning;
> Great is Your faithfulness.
> "The Lord is my portion," says my soul,
> "Therefore I hope in Him!"
> The Lord is good to those who wait for Him,
> To the soul who seeks Him (Lamentations 3:21–25).

God's love, mercy, and faithfulness never cease, no matter how bad things get. And life can get bad, really bad. Both Christians and non-Christians can go through very dark, tragic experiences. But Christians who places their trust and faith in Jesus will have hope, just as Jeremiah wrote in Lamentations. They will have hope when all seems lost; hope when no light can be seen; hope when pain engulfs the soul; and hope in the darkest, most agonizing moments of life!

In those dark moments, we may think that God has lost sight of us; somehow, we have fallen through the cracks of God's floorboards, or the enemy's onslaught has somehow hidden us from God's view. Trauma can seem to isolate us and send us into some lonely places that no human sees or seems to care about. It may seem as though even God does not know or understand the deep aching wounds that have been inflicted on us.

For years, David fled for his life as King Saul became more and more obsessed with hatred and jealousy of him. In fact, King Saul dedicated the latter part of his life to hunting down David so he could destroy him. Yet David rejoiced in God's loving-kindness. He said, "I will be glad and rejoice in Your mercy, for You have considered my trouble; You have known my soul in adversities" (Psalm 31:7). And later he penned the beautiful, poetic words in Psalm 139:1–10:

> O LORD, You have searched me and known me.
> You know my sitting down and my rising up;
> You understand my thought afar off.
> You comprehend my path and my lying down,
> And are acquainted with all my ways.
> For there is not a word on my tongue,
> But behold, O LORD, You know it altogether.
> You have hedged me behind and before,
> And laid Your hand upon me.
> Such knowledge is too wonderful for me;
> It is high, I cannot attain it.
> Where can I go from Your Spirit?
> Or where can I flee from Your presence?
> If I ascend into heaven, You are there;
> If I make my bed in hell, behold, You are there.
> If I take the wings of the morning,
> And dwell in the uttermost parts of the sea,
> Even there Your hand shall lead me,
> And Your right hand shall hold me.

There is something immensely comforting about knowing that Someone understands and feels our deepest pain and that we are not alone in our trouble. *God sees us!* And troubles are not brought into our lives by a malicious God. Such a concept is an invention of Satan, who has been wonderfully successful in propagating it. No matter what circumstances we find ourselves in, we can be fully convinced that God's love for us never ceases. The Bible affirms this great truth triumphantly!

Seen and heard

Hagar was Sarai's personal maid. She found herself caught up in a twisted plan to bring about what God had promised to fulfill for Abram.* The promise from God was that Sarai and Abram would have a son. But, as it turned out, Sarai did not seem to be able to have children (Genesis 16:1). In order to fulfill God's plan, she suggested that they take matters into their own hands. Abram would have sex with Sarai's handmaiden, Hagar, whose child could then become the child of promise. It seemed like a brilliant idea! They carried out the plan, and Hagar became pregnant. As one might expect, jealousy soon set in, and Sarai dealt very harshly with Hagar, who soon fled from her. But God intervened in Hagar's flight.

Who would hear the anguish of this lowly Egyptian maid? Who would be her advocate? God would. He told her,

"I will multiply your descendants exceedingly. . . .

"Behold, you are with child,
And you shall bear a son.
You shall call his name Ishmael,
Because the LORD has heard your affliction" (verses 10, 11).

There "she called the name of the LORD who spoke to her, You-Are-the-God-Who-Sees" (verse 13), who in Hebrew, is *El Roi*.

Later, after God fulfilled the promise of a son (Isaac) for Abraham *through Sarah*, as He had said He would do from the very beginning, Sarah wanted Hagar and her son, Ishmael, cast away because she did not want Ishmael to be an heir along with her son, Isaac. So even

---

* Later, God changed their names from Abram to Abraham and Sarai to Sarah (Genesis 17:5, 15).

though it grieved Abraham much, he sent Hagar and Ishmael away into the wilderness.

Hagar had been caught in the middle of a selfish plan. Now she and her son, Ishmael, had been cast away. They had become unwanted, yet God saw her and made provision for her again. He even made a special promise to her, saying that her son would also be the father of a great nation (Genesis 21:17, 18).

What does Psalm 147:3 say about God? "He heals the brokenhearted and binds up their wounds." The story of Hagar clearly demonstrates that God hears the cries of the afflicted and the "unwanted." He sees those who are alone and wounded, and He brings promises and healing to them.

This world constantly throws out all sorts of challenges at us. Through these troubles, Satan is trying to disrupt every journey God sets His children on. Satan is trying to throw us into a mental state of doubt and fear, causing us to veer off track and send us into a ditch of despair, where we will be lost and confused, thinking we are alone and abandoned. Satan's ultimate goal is to convince us that *if* God is a merciful God, then He will not let bad things happen to us. And because bad things are happening to us, then God must not be trustworthy.

The truth is, God is right there with us, helping us along the troublesome way. We may not always know what God is doing or how He is working, but because we trust in His grace and mercy. We can know for certain that He cares for us and that He is working on our behalf. *Even without knowing the details of why bad things happen to us, we can know that God is for us, no matter what we may have to go through.*

As we conclude this chapter, I want to share a poem by Oliver Wendell Holmes, which ranks high among my favorites.

> O Love Divine, that stooped to share
>   Our sharpest pang, our bitterest tear,
> On Thee we cast each earthborn care,
>   We smile at pain while Thou art near!

Though long the weary way we tread,
    And sorrow crown each lingering year,
No path we shun, no darkness dread,
    Our hearts still whispering, Thou art near!

When drooping pleasure turns to grief,
    And trembling faith is changed to fear,
The murmuring wind, the quivering leaf
    Shall softly tell us, Thou art near!

On Thee we fling our burdening woe,
    O Love Divine, forever dear;
Content to suffer, while we know,
    Living and dying, Thou art near![1]

---

1. Oliver Wendell Holmes Sr., "Hymn of Trust," in *The Professor at the Breakfast-Table,* Riverside Edition (New York: Houghton, Mifflin, 1895), 282.

Chapter 7

The Good Shepherd

In John 10:1–4, Jesus tells us,

"I assure you and most solemnly say to you, he who does not enter by the door into the sheepfold, but climbs up from some other place [on the stone wall], that one is a thief and a robber. But he who enters by the door is the shepherd of the sheep [the protector and provider]. The doorkeeper opens [the gate] for this man, and the sheep hear his voice and pay attention to it. And [knowing that they listen] he calls his own sheep by name and leads them out [to pasture]. When he has brought all his own sheep outside, he walks on ahead of them, and the sheep follow him because they know his voice and recognize his call" (AMP).

For whom does the sheep gate open? The door of the sheepfold opens *only to* Jesus, the Good Shepherd, and to those who hear Jesus' invitation and accept it.

Jesus continues, "I am the Door for the sheep [leading to life]. All who came before Me [as false messiahs and self-appointed leaders] are thieves and robbers, but the [true] sheep did not hear them. I am the Door; anyone who enters through Me will be saved [and will live forever], and will go in and out [freely], and find pasture (spiritual security)" (verses 7–9, AMP).

What did Jesus say He was? He is the door. So all who want to enter the path that leads to life must first go to Jesus. This is quite wonderful because, as we learned in the previous chapters, Jesus is our greatest need and our greatest help through this life.

This path that Jesus leads us on is not a one-size-fits-all kind of trail. This is a very *personalized* trail, designed by a very *personal* Savior.

It is crucial to understand that the One who grants us entrance also walks and talks with us along the way. Never are we left alone to do our own problem solving. On this path, a special, deep, and meaningful relationship is meant to develop between us as pilgrims and Jesus our Guide.

If this walking, talking relationship does not occur and deepen, there is a breakdown of cooperation and teamwork, revealing a conflict of interests. It is a sad fact that many who think they are walking on God's path actually do not even know God. And there are characteristics in their lives that reveal that the connection they claim to have with God is broken.

Astounding as it may seem, professed followers of Jesus may do many wonderful things in His name without really knowing Him. Matthew 7:21–23 says, "Not everyone who says to Me, 'Lord, Lord,' shall enter the kingdom of heaven, but he who *does the will of My Father* in heaven. Many will say to Me in that day, 'Lord, Lord, have we not prophesied in Your name, cast out demons in Your name, and done many wonders in Your name?' And then I will declare to them, 'I never knew you; depart from Me, you who practice lawlessness!' " (emphasis added).

Jesus continues to explain, "Beware of false prophets, who come to you in sheep's clothing, but inwardly they are ravenous wolves. You will know them by their fruits. Do men gather grapes from thornbushes or figs from thistles? Even so, every good tree bears good fruit, but a bad tree bears bad fruit. A good tree cannot bear bad fruit, nor can a bad tree bear good fruit" (verses 15–18).

Here Jesus warns us to be aware that not every person is really who he or she claims to be. I feel that it is important to make the distinction clear between a true believer and a professed believer.

Unfortunately, it is often the ones who profess to be followers of Jesus who misrepresent the character of God and cause undue confusion about who God's people are supposed to be, wounding innocent victims along the way. Many make claims all day about their faith in God, but they consistently and frequently reveal, through their actions and words, that they are not living lives of faith and obedience.

Though a committed, surrendered Christian will have failures and shortcomings, there should be a consistently humble walk of obedience. And if this honest Christian stumbles, there should be a spirit of repentance and confession, not just toward God but toward those this person has sinned against.

Obviously, Jesus intends for those walking the straight and narrow path to have a growing, abiding relationship with Him, *doing the will of the Father* in heaven (verses 13, 14, 21). With every victorious experience in one's walk with Jesus, faith grows and trust deepens.

Speaking about His own people, God says, "When they came to the nations, wherever they went, they profaned My holy name—when they said of them, 'These are the people of the Lord, and yet they have gone out of His land.' But I had concern for My holy name, which the house of Israel had profaned among the nations wherever they went" (Ezekiel 36:20, 21).

Later in Ezekiel 36, God says that He will restore the holiness of His name by restoring His people to holiness (verses 26–29). If they are willing to receive God's transforming power in their lives, He promises to give them new hearts and new spirits and cause them to walk in His ways. This is a beautiful picture of God's transformative power in a person's life. It is *His power, His work,* and *His righteousness* that will be manifested in the believer's life. In other words, the fruit of God's work will be evident in him or her.

Take note of this wonderful verse in 2 Corinthians that reveals the pilgrim progressing and being transformed as he walks with Jesus: "But we all, with unveiled face, beholding as in a mirror the glory of the Lord, are being transformed into the same image from glory to glory, just as by the Spirit of the Lord" (2 Corinthians 3:18).

God's leading *into* tough times

The Good Shepherd has a specific plan for those of us who want to hear His voice and walk His path. As He leads us, He wants to transform us more and more into His image (that is, into representing and reflecting His character). To develop this kind of transformation in us, God designs a path for each of us that may look very different from what we first expected. Let us consider Psalm 66:10–12:

> For You, O God, have tested us;
> You have refined us as silver is refined.
> You brought us into the net;
> You laid affliction on our backs.
> You have caused men to ride over our heads;
> We went through fire and through water;
> But You brought us out to rich fulfillment.

This psalm reveals that instead of diverting our path around the traps, the fires, and the floods, God leads us *into* and *through them*. As shocking as it may sound at first, it is true. God leads His dear children into all sorts of difficult times! The best way to understand this is to read a few of the examples in the Bible.

King Darius put 120 princes over his kingdom to deal with the affairs of the land. Over those men, he put three presidents. Of the three presidents, Daniel was the leader. The king specifically preferred Daniel above the others because "an excellent spirit was in him; and the king gave thought to setting him over the whole realm" (Daniel 6:3). But this provoked the jealously of the presidents and princes below him. They sought to find fault with Daniel, but they could not find anything because "he was faithful" (verse 4). This made them all the more determined to destroy him.

They knew he worshiped Jehovah, the God of Israel, and he was very dedicated and faithful to his God. So the presidents and princes thought that if they could devise a plan that forced Daniel to choose between the law of his God and the law of King Darius, then they could accuse him of treason. They correctly assumed that he would choose allegiance to his God over allegiance to the king.

Daniel 6:7 tells us that they went before the king and said, "All the governors of the kingdom . . . have consulted together to establish a royal statute and to make a firm decree, that whoever petitions any god or man for thirty days, except you, O king, shall be cast into the den of lions."

Who laid the trap for Daniel? These men, caught up in the clutches of jealousy, laid this cruel net for Daniel. Even the king did not know what was going on as they beguiled him with their deceptive words. He failed to see the implications of such a ridiculous law. Flattered, "King Darius signed the written decree" (verse 9).

Daniel responded with courage. "Now when Daniel knew that the writing was signed, he went home. And in his upper room, with his windows open toward Jerusalem, he knelt down on his knees three times that day, and prayed and gave thanks before his God, as was his custom since early days" (verse 10).

When Daniel knew what had happened, what did he do? He immediately took the matter to God in prayer! Did he hide so that no one could see him praying? No! Daniel knew the consequences of praying to God openly, but he would not be intimidated by men and their unjust laws. He sought God all the more and trusted that He would take care of him.

Do you think Daniel asked God to save him from the lions' den? I know that would have been my prayer! Even Jesus prayed a prayer like that just before He faced the darkest time in His life. Jesus knelt down to pray, saying, "Father, if it is Your will, take this cup away from Me" (Luke 22:42). The trial before Him was so dark, so painful, and so intense that He sweat drops of blood as He prayed (verse 44)!

When faced with tremendous troubles, pain, and perhaps even death, our humanity, in its frailty and weakness, cries out, No! Please, no! I do not want to go forward into the trials ahead!

It is natural to resist suffering and balk at anything that would cause us pain. Our Savior intimately understood what that felt like, but He continued His prayer with these triumphant words of trust:

"Nevertheless, not My will, but Yours, be done" (verse 42). Jesus trusted His Father. Even though He did not want to drink the cup of suffering and death that was ahead of Him, He consented to remain in His Father's hands and will. Jesus would drink whatever cup the Father placed before Him because He trusted that His Father knew best.

Next time you are faced with hard times and unjust cruelty (perhaps that is your situation right now), remember Jesus' example: "I don't want to, but if it is God's will that I have to, then I will." Even though you may have to go through some very tough and challenging times, you can know that God will provide everything you need to face the challenge.

Jesus, knowing that Peter would stumble and fail the very same test by denying Him three times, said to him, "Watch and pray, lest you enter into temptation. The spirit indeed is willing, but the flesh is weak" (Mark 14:38). Oh, how we all know the weaknesses of the flesh! I am sure we can all echo what Paul wrote in Romans 7:18, 19: "For I know that in me (that is, in my flesh) nothing good dwells; for to will is present with me, but how to perform what is good I do not find. For the good that I will to do, I do not do; but the evil I will not to do, that I practice." Frustrating, isn't it?

That is why Jesus was so earnest in directing Peter to pray. When we see storm clouds form and grow more and more menacing, it is surely a time to pray! Pray for strength, and pray for power! The presence of the Holy Spirit in our lives enables us to live for Jesus. Romans 8:5 tells us, "For those who live according to the flesh set their minds on the things of the flesh, but those who live according to the Spirit, the things of the Spirit." Galatians 5:16 says, "I say then: Walk in the Spirit, and you shall not fulfill the lust of the flesh"; "let us also walk in the Spirit" (verse 25). The truth is, if we walk forward in the flesh, timid and weak, we will not get very far before we fall. The only way to move forward with confidence into an hour of temptation and trial is to walk forward in prayer and faith and in the power of the Spirit!

Mercy in the trap

Well, what about Daniel? What happened to him? All the princes and presidents went before the king and reminded him of the law he had signed. "Have you not signed a decree that every man who petitions any god or man within thirty days, except you, O king, shall be cast into the den of lions?" (Daniel 6:12). The king acknowledged that they were correct and that the law, according to the Medes and the Persians, could not be changed!

Then, gleefully, they reported that Daniel had sought his God in prayer three times a day, irrespective of the king's decree. When the king heard what they said, his eyes were opened to their deceit. He argued with them, but they reminded him that his laws could not be changed as he himself had stated. He labored all day, trying to find ways to free Daniel, but he could not.

So according to the law, Daniel had to be thrown into the lions' den. We might easily wonder how God could let that happen to His faithful servant. Surely God saw the trap, yet He did not stop it from happening! The truth is, God deliberately brought Daniel into the net, just like Psalm 66:11 says, "You brought us into the net; you laid affliction on our backs."

When we are in "the net," Satan uses every trick in the book to make us doubt God's guidance and wisdom. He wants us to start playing the blame game against God and label Him as enemy number one! "It's all *God's* fault!" Satan wants to make us believe that if God really cared about us, then He wouldn't lead us into a trap. *God wouldn't do something like that, would He?*

But even though God brought Daniel into a dark hole filled with hungry beasts, He did not let him die. Daniel's triumphant testimony was this: "My God sent His angel and shut the lions' mouths" (Daniel 6:22). And everyone knew he was telling the truth because he lived to tell about it! Read what the king announced about Daniel's God in Daniel 6:25–27:

Then King Darius wrote:

To all peoples, nations, and languages that dwell in all the earth:
Peace be multiplied to you.
I make a decree that in every dominion of my kingdom men must tremble and fear before the God of Daniel.

> For He is the living God,
> And steadfast forever;
> His kingdom is the one which shall not be destroyed,
> And His dominion shall endure to the end.
> He delivers and rescues,
> And He works signs and wonders
> In heaven and on earth,
> Who has delivered Daniel from the power of the lions.

I delight in the way in which the loving, merciful character of Daniel's God was put on public display throughout the entire kingdom! When, for a moment, the outcome looked really bad (I mean, could it have gotten any worse?), it sure seemed like a time to doubt God and throw one's faith aside. But God was *not finished yet*. And that is perhaps the crucial thing to remember when we find ourselves in a trap, wondering why God did not divert us around it. This brings to mind the Israelite's situation, pinched between the Red Sea and the Egyptian army. Even then, God had a plan for the Israelites. He had a plan for Daniel. And He has a plan now, for each of us. Remember, He is not finished with us yet. Do not throw in the towel too soon! Wait on the Lord. As David reminds us,

> The LORD is my shepherd;
> I shall not want.
> He makes me to lie down in green pastures;
> He leads me beside the still waters.
> He restores my soul;
> He leads me in the paths of righteousness
> For His name's sake.
> Yea, though I walk through the valley of the shadow of death,

I will fear no evil;
For You are with me;
Your rod and Your staff, they comfort me.
You prepare a table before me in the presence of my enemies;
You anoint my head with oil;
My cup runs over.
Surely goodness and mercy shall follow me
All the days of my life;
And I will dwell in the house of the LORD
Forever (Psalm 23).

God led David, the writer of this psalm, through the valley of the shadow of death on several occasions. It is important to note that God does not always keep us on the mountain's top. He leads us all over the place—in the green meadows, by still waters, through the dark and deep valleys, into the presence of our enemies, and into the storm.

During the dark times, it may be hard to see God leading us, but David compared God's care for us to the care of a faithful shepherd for his sheep. When we have to travel through the darkness, God is with us, for His rod and His staff comfort us. A gentle tap of the shepherd's staff would tell his sheep, "It's OK; I am still here." A tender correcting maneuver of his rod would keep them on the right path. We may not be able to see clearly in the dark, but God can! He sees the entire path as clear as day, so all we need is to learn to lean on Him for guidance.

Chapter 8

In the Fire

Daniel's three friends, Shadrach, Meshach, and Abed-Nego, also experienced a life-and-death trial like Daniel did, except in their case, it was a prideful king with a fiery furnace. The king of Babylon, Nebuchadnezzar, wanted to make a public display of his conviction that his kingdom would last forever. So he decided to make a colossal statue of himself that was ninety feet high and nine feet wide. He commanded all the subjects in his kingdom to come and see it (Daniel 3:1–3).

On the day the statue was to be displayed, all the populace was there, awestruck by this colossal statue. But this presented a serious problem for God's faithful followers—Shadrach, Meshach, and Abed-Nego. The problem was that everyone was commanded to bow down and worship the statue when the music played. And the punishment for not bowing down in worship would be death in a fiery furnace (verses 4–6). Therefore, Daniel's three friends had a problem because their God, Yahweh, was the only God they were going to bow down to and worship.

Well, Daniel 3:12 tells us that their refusal to bow down to the golden image was brought to the king's attention: "There are certain Jews whom you have set over the affairs of the province of Babylon: Shadrach, Meshach, and Abed-Nego; these men, O king, have not paid due regard to you. They do not serve your gods or worship the gold image which you have set up."

Sometimes God's people find themselves in precarious situations that call for extraordinary faith in an extraordinary God. At these times, their faith and loyalty to God are publicly tested, even to the point of disobeying the laws of the land in order to stand true to God.

Shadrach, Meshach, and Abed-Nego were hauled before the angry king. First, what they were supposed to do was made clear to them, just in case they had misunderstood. But this was not a matter of confusion on their part; it was a matter of faith, loyalty, and obedience to *their God, no matter the cost*! They were also told, in no uncertain terms, what the result of continued disobedience to the king's order would be.

Facing extreme pressure as they stood before the angry king, what did Shadrach, Meshach, and Abed-Nego tell the king they would not do? Daniel 3:18 tells us what they said: "Let it be known to you, O king, that we do not serve your gods, nor will we worship the gold image which you have set up."

Of course, this angered the king tremendously. Daniel 3:19–23 records his response:

> Then Nebuchadnezzar was full of fury.... *He spoke and commanded that they heat the furnace seven times more than it was usually heated.* And he commanded certain mighty men of valor who were in his army to bind Shadrach, Meshach, and Abed-Nego, and cast them into the burning fiery furnace. Then these men were bound in their coats, their trousers, their turbans, and their other garments, and were cast into the midst of the burning fiery furnace. Therefore, because the king's command was urgent, and the furnace exceedingly hot, the flame of the fire killed those men who took up Shadrach, Meshach, and Abed-Nego. And these three men, Shadrach, Meshach, and Abed-Nego, fell down bound into the midst of the burning fiery furnace (emphasis added).

There was no way anyone could survive such an intense flame—unless God was on their side, and in this case, He was! The account continues:

King Nebuchadnezzar was astonished; and he rose in haste and spoke, saying to his counselors, "Did we not cast three men bound into the midst of the fire?"

They answered and said to the king, "True, O king."

"Look!" he answered, "I see four men loose, walking in the midst of the fire; and they are not hurt, and the form of the fourth is like the Son of God" (verses 24, 25).

God's path for these men led them into a trap, a fiery furnace, and safely out the other side. Who would have thought that God would lead some of His faithful children through such terrifying circumstances? It is inevitable that some of God's people will find themselves pinned between two choices: (1) to faithfully continue to follow God, or (2) to obey the dictates of earthly governments. To continue to follow God could mean a fiery test and trial, but we can take comfort in the fact that God will be with us through it all.

Blessings in the fire

How many times do we pray for protection, safe travels, and smooth sailing? *All the time.* Who wants to travel a road of suffering? Oftentimes we think that if we have safe travels, plenty to eat, and a comfortable living, then we are blessed. And we are blessed! But the fact that God sometimes leads His children into all sorts of uncomfortable circumstances does not mean that His blessings have stopped coming our way.

In Isaiah 43:1, 2, we read,

> But now, thus says the LORD, who created you, O Jacob,
> And He who formed you, O Israel:
> "Fear not, for I have redeemed you;
> I have called you by your name;
> You are Mine.
> When you pass through the waters, *I will be with you*;
> And through the rivers, they shall not overflow you.
> When you walk through the fire, you shall not be burned,

Nor shall the flame scorch you" (emphasis added).

The key word I want everyone to see here is *when*. It is not that you will *never* go through the flood or the fire. It is *when* you do, *God will be with you.* That is a promise of an enormous blessing that must not be overlooked. When God's path leads us into the flood and into the fire and into the storm and into tribulation, He promises to bless us with His presence, just as He was present with Shadrach, Meshach, and Abed-Nego.

Hebrews 13:5 reassures us that "He has said, 'I WILL NEVER [under any circumstances] DESERT YOU [nor give you up nor leave you without support, nor will I in any degree leave you helpless], NOR WILL I FORSAKE or LET YOU DOWN or RELAX MY HOLD ON YOU [assuredly not]!' " (AMP). I love this promise! It is a statement that can inspire us with utmost confidence and assurance. Let me just outline it again:

- I will not desert you.
- I will not give you up.
- I will not leave you without support.
- I will not leave you helpless.
- I will not forsake you.
- I will not let you go.

And if that was not enough, Deuteronomy 31:6 says, "Be strong and of good courage, do not fear nor be afraid of them; for the LORD your God, He is the One who goes with you. He will not leave you nor forsake you." We can add to that list:

- I will not fail you.
- I will go with you.

As God's people travel the narrow path, we have a Companion that nonbelievers do not have. Like I said earlier, the path God leads His people on is a special, personalized trail, designed by a very personal Savior. All through the Bible, we see God's people experience a lot of trouble in their lives. Our omniscient God saw it all and led them *through* every trial. Many of these tough times were major, life-altering events. But God never led them there to leave them there. He would bring them through that trial.

When my sister and I were in our teens, we built a formidable sledding trail behind our house in Alaska. It was steep and went through the thick woods. At first glance, it did not really look like a sledding trail—you know, the ones that go in a straight line down a gentle slope. This trail twisted and turned, jolted us this way and that around all sorts of woodland obstacles that we certainly did not want to run into.

We could steer down that hill at lightning speed through the woods with precision and mastery. We knew how to lean with our bodies and steer with our hands to turn the sled. A twist of our hips would throw the back end of the sled around a corner as fast as we needed to. Negotiating this trail successfully required a lot of knowledge and skill.

We knew every bump, every jump, and every turn because we had designed it, planned it, and created what we considered to be the very best route. If you did not know how to maneuver this sledding trail, you would not get very far before you got into trouble. You would need to learn how to use the sled and move your body in a coordinated way. You would need guidance and instruction from the one who knew the way, from the one who planned the route, and from the one who carved the trail. It would not be easy; in fact, it would be downright frightening at times. But if you listened to the one who knew what was ahead, down the trail, the next turn, the drop-off, the bush, the tree, the roots, the rocks—if you listened and trusted your guides you would make it through successfully. That is not to say that you would not bruise a knee or lose a glove. You might get smacked by a bush or momentarily be blinded by snow, but you would get through it.

Take note of what Revelation 21:6, 7 says: "And He said to me, 'It is done! I am the Alpha and the Omega, the Beginning and the

End. I will give of the fountain of the water of life freely to him who thirsts. He who overcomes shall inherit all things, and I will be his God and he shall be My [child].' "

What does "the Alpha and the Omega" mean? It means that God is the beginning and the end. There is not one detail that is hidden from His view. He sees it all. He knows it all. He is *omniscient*, which means He knows everything. This being the case, Has He not seen your path? Has He not seen your falling and your rising? Has He not seen all things behind you, all things you are going through now, and all things ahead of you? With careful planning, He has designed your path. He has seen the different outcomes of your choices and created the best route through the troubles you will face. Some troubles He will take out of the way, let you skirt around, or even thwart. At other times, He sees that the best way for you is through the fire and through the flood. You will need His constant instruction and guidance to negotiate this kind of treacherous path successfully.

Chapter 9

When the Path Ends

We have read how God saved Daniel from being eaten alive. We have read how his three friends went through a fiery furnace but were not burned. We caught a glimpse of David going through the valley of the shadow of death without dying. These victories may make us believe that even though God may lead us into places of great danger, we will come out of dangerous situations alive every time. But unless Jesus returns first, one day each person's life will cease, and his or her path will end. In Hebrews 11:32–35, we read, "And what more shall I say? For the time would fail me to tell of Gideon and Barak and Samson and Jephthah, also of David and Samuel and the prophets: who through faith subdued kingdoms, worked righteousness, obtained promises, stopped the mouths of lions, quenched the violence of fire, escaped the edge of the sword, out of weakness were made strong, became valiant in battle, turned to flight the armies of the aliens. Women received their dead raised to life again."

After Hebrews 11's long list of men and women who, "by faith," followed God wherever He led them and were victorious as a result, we get to the end of the list, and admittedly, it starts sounding a bit alarming. Continuing on, we read, "Others were tortured, not accepting deliverance, that they might obtain a better resurrection. Still others had trial of mockings and scourgings, yes, and of chains and imprisonment. They were stoned, they were sawn in two, were tempted, were slain with the sword. They wandered about in sheepskins and goatskins, being destitute, afflicted, tormented—of whom the world was not worthy. They wandered in deserts and mountains, in dens and caves of the earth" (verses 35–38).

Again, God's people followed "by faith," but this time they suffered torture, stoning, being sawn in half, being slain by the sword—*what is going on here?* Those are certainly not my idea of wonderful journeys or happy endings! Here we see that God's people of faith may lose their lives in all sorts of cruel ways. So when God's people face death, at the end of the day, when all is said and done, what do Christians have that non-Christians do not have? The answer is *hope*!

Let us consider the story of Lazarus. When Lazarus became sick, his sisters, Mary and Martha, sent Jesus word about his sickness. Now Jesus loved Lazarus as a dear friend, but for some reason, He did not do anything after receiving the news of His friend's sickness. A few days later Jesus decided to go to Lazarus's house, saying to His disciples, "Lazarus is dead" (John 11:14). *Why did Jesus wait?* This is a legitimate question to ask. Martha knew that her "brother would not have died" if Jesus had come sooner (verse 21). In response, Jesus said in simple words, "Your brother will rise again" (verse 23).

Pause for a moment. Do you hear, do you feel the agonizing, grief-stricken heart questioning why Jesus had not come sooner, why He had waited, and why He had not done anything to stop her brother from dying? But do you also hear Jesus' triumphant, unwavering statement that Martha would see her brother alive again?

Jesus said to Martha, "I am the resurrection and the life. He who believes in Me, though he may die, he shall live. And whoever lives and believes in Me shall never die. Do you believe this?" (verses 25, 26). This means that Jesus has the power to raise the dead and restore life. After all, He came that we "may have life" (John 10:10).

> "For I have come down from heaven, not to do My own will, but the will of Him who sent Me. This is the will of the Father who sent Me, that of all He has given Me I should lose nothing, but should raise it up at the last day. And this is the will of Him who sent Me, that everyone who sees the Son and believes in Him may

have everlasting life; and I will raise him up at the last day.". . .

. . . "No one can come to Me unless the Father who sent Me draws him; and I will raise him up at the last day.". . .

. . . "Whoever eats My flesh and drinks My blood has eternal life, and I will raise him up at the last day" (John 6:38–40, 44, 54).

When will Jesus resurrect those who have died? Four times in this passage, Jesus affirms that He will raise up those who have died "at the last day." Even though our journey on this earth may end, a new journey will begin when Jesus resurrects us to life again, *at the last day.*

This last-day resurrection hope is given specifically to Christians. If we die with faith in Jesus and the hope He provides, trusting that God has a plan, trusting that He has provided something better for us, trusting that He has prepared an eternal city for us, and trusting that He can and will raise us up in the last day, then we have nothing to fear! Our last day here on this earth is not God's last day for us; it is not the end of the story. God has determined that we will live eternally with Him.

There will come a time when "God will wipe away every tear from their eyes; there shall be no more death, nor sorrow, nor crying. There shall be no more pain, for the former things have passed away" (Revelation 21:4).

You may have friends and family members who have died, and to you, they did not appear to be saved by Jesus or did not appear to believe in Jesus. What about them? We do not know their final choice. Only Jesus knows the heart of every individual, and we must leave the end results in His hands, trusting in His infinite wisdom. One thing we can know for sure, one thing we can rest in is hope— hope that we may see our loved ones again at the resurrection of the faithful at the last day.

Death is always a difficult subject to discuss because death is so final and the results of another person's life and choices are so unknown, *but God knows*, and we can leave the final judgment with Him and trust His wisdom, mercy, and grace.

We all have to run the race and walk the path *that has been set before us*. As we travel, where are we to look? Hebrews reminds us,

> Therefore, since we are surrounded by so great a cloud of witnesses [who by faith have testified to the truth of God's absolute faithfulness], stripping off every unnecessary weight and the sin which so easily and cleverly entangles us, let us run with endurance and active persistence the race that is set before us, [looking away from all that will distract us and] focusing our eyes on Jesus, who is the Author and Perfecter of faith [the first incentive for our belief and the One who brings our faith to maturity], who for the joy [of accomplishing the goal] set before Him endured the cross, disregarding the shame, and sat down at the right hand of the throne of God [revealing His deity, His authority, and the completion of His work] (Hebrews 12:1, 2, AMP).

The *Author* and the *Finisher*

The Bible is filled with wonderful stories of people whose lives reflected Jesus' influence. Our journey in this life is also like a story. As He leads us, we can trust that He is writing our story of faith, too, even through the difficult times. Jesus is the Author *and* Finisher of our faith, which means He has the final word and the closing statement. He is in charge of completing our life story.

In Hebrews 11, the theme is "by faith" _____ [God's follower] did _____ [short phrase or summary of what each person was known for]. Today, by faith, you can move forward, trusting God, no matter what He leads you through so that you will be remembered for your faithfulness in this life and in the book of life (Revelation 3:5). Again, the author of Hebrews counsels us: "Just consider and meditate on Him who endured from sinners such bitter hostility against Himself [consider it all in comparison with your trials], so that you will not grow weary and lose heart" (Hebrews 12:3, AMP).

It is easy to become overwhelmed and wearied, thinking that we cannot endure. Hebrews 12:3 tells us to consider Jesus, who endured test and trial *just like us*. As we read His story, we are to gain encouragement and strength from Him who experienced violence, unfairness, and troubles in His life—*just like we do.*

Remember, Jesus told the disciples to go to the other side of the lake, and they arrived there. Remember, God freed the Israelites from slavery and pledged to bring them to the Promised Land, and they arrived there. Now He has promised to bring you to a precious destination as well—eternity with Him! So believe that you also can and will arrive there! Jesus promised us, "Let not your heart be troubled; you believe in God, believe also in Me. In My Father's house are many mansions; if it were not so, I would have told you. I go to prepare a place for you. And if I go and prepare a place for you, I will come again and receive you to Myself; that where I am, there you may be also" (John 14:1–3).

God is preparing a special place for us. Will He come again? Yes! Why is He coming again? He is coming again to get us and take us with Him so that we can dwell with Him for eternity.

This does not mean our lives on this earth may not end before Jesus comes back. They may, but if we are faithful, God's promise stands sure. Should we die before His second coming, He will raise us up and take us to that final destination—heaven—so that where He is, we will be as well.

We have hope! We have nothing to fear!

Chapter 10

Decisions and Consequences

Joseph was a teenager when he excitedly described his first notable dream to his brothers, "There we were, binding sheaves in the field. Then behold, my sheaf arose and also stood upright; and indeed your sheaves stood all around and bowed down to my sheaf" (Genesis 37:6, 7). Now Joseph's brothers did not like him, and the dreams he shared with them intensified their dislike. He, their baby brother, was insinuating that they, his older brothers, would bow down to him?

Part of the reason they did not like him was that he was a tattletale. When his brothers did evil things, Joseph would tell their dad (verse 2), and that really angered them. Most children have probably had that experience with siblings, cousins, or playmates. Do you remember a time when you did something you definitely should not have done, and someone told on you? Oh, the anger that resulted! No one likes to be told on.

But that was only half of their reason for disliking their little brother. It was obvious that Joseph was the favorite son of Jacob: "Israel [Jacob] loved Joseph more than all his children, because he was the son of his old age" (verse 3). To show his son his extra fondness, he had a coat of many colors made for him. This act of favoritism made his brothers really despise him!

And then Joseph had a second dream, which he told to everyone: "Look, I have dreamed another dream. And this time, the sun, the moon, and the eleven stars bowed down to me" (verse 9).

On hearing about this dream, even his father rebuked him. "What is this dream that you have dreamed? Shall your mother and I and your brothers indeed come to bow down to the earth before you?" (verse 10).

As the story goes, Jacob sent Joseph out to check on his brothers, who were in the fields, watching the flocks. "Now when they saw him afar off, even before he came near them, they conspired against him to kill him. Then they said to one another, 'Look, this dreamer is coming! Come therefore, let us now kill him and cast him into some pit; and we shall say, "Some wild beast has devoured him." We shall see what will become of his dreams!' " (verses 18–20).

When Joseph's brothers saw him, what did they plan among themselves to do with him? Murder!

Reuben, one of the brothers, did not like the sound of murder, and he suggested that they throw Joseph in a pit in the wilderness. Reuben secretly wanted to rescue the boy and bring him back to his dad. When Joseph came near, the brothers stripped him of his coat of many colors and threw him into a pit.

> They sat down to eat a meal. Then they lifted their eyes and looked, and there was a company of Ishmaelites, coming from Gilead with their camels, bearing spices, balm, and myrrh, on their way to carry them down to Egypt. So Judah said to his brothers, "What profit is there if we kill our brother and conceal his blood? Come and let us sell him to the Ishmaelites, and let not our hand be upon him, for he is our brother and our flesh." And his brothers listened. Then Midianite traders passed by; so the brothers pulled Joseph up and lifted him out of the pit, and sold him to the Ishmaelites for twenty shekels of silver. And they took Joseph to Egypt.
>
> Then Reuben returned to the pit, and indeed Joseph was not in the pit; and he tore his clothes (verses 25–29).

Apparently, Reuben was not there when the plan of selling Joseph was carried out. When he went to the pit to rescue his little brother and saw that Joseph was no longer there, he was extremely distraught and remorseful. Reuben grabbed the clothing over his chest and tore it in half to express his grief (verse 29).

The brothers, on the other hand, were unfazed. They calmly proceeded to kill a goat and splatter the goat's blood over Joseph's coat of many colors. Then they returned home and told their dad that they had found the coat and did not know whether it was Joseph's (verses 32–34). Jacob knew it was his little boy's coat, and he tore his clothing in sorrow and deep grief, just as Reuben had done.

Joseph was betrayed and sold by his own brothers. What do you think was going through that seventeen-year-old's mind as he was carried off to Egypt? It must have been dreadful!

Joseph was young. Maybe he did not realize the depth of his brothers hostility and jealousy. Most likely he did not fully think about the results of his words and how they might have seemed arrogant. If he had realized that broadcasting his dreams would push his brothers over the edge, he probably would not have told them at all!

To be fair, Joseph's tumble into the angry arms of his brothers wasn't *all* his fault. His brothers could have made better choices too. In fact, the act of getting rid of him fell strictly upon their shoulders. They were to blame for that final, fateful choice of selling Joseph as a slave. It was their choice, and they were plain wrong.

The enemy is working ceaselessly to destroy us on many fronts and from different angles. When he tempts us to act unwisely, his victory is all the more terrible if, as a consequence, he can tempt others to respond to our carelessness with revengeful rage, like Joseph's brothers ended up doing. We have all experienced this when a reckless remark or careless action has blown up into a bigger mess.

James understood this when he said,

> The tongue is a little member and boasts great things.
> See how great a forest a little fire kindles! (James 3:5).

One little spark is known to have burned down an entire forest. Similarly, in speaking about a false teaching that had made its way into the Galatian churches, Paul wrote, "A little leaven leavens the whole lump" (Galatians 5:9). In other words, it takes only a little bit of yeast to make a whole loaf of bread rise. Spiritually speaking, a slight doctrinal error can mislead an entire church. Little words and actions can combine into a really big disaster—which is what happened with Joseph and his brothers—creating a disaster so big that it changes people's lives forever.

A tumble into calamity usually involves more than just ourselves and our personal choices. Clearly, we are not always to blame for every bad thing that happens to us. Sometimes, however, our own choices lead us into affliction, misery, and much sorrow. Sometimes our decisions are not merely careless but actually bad, and those bad decisions often have serious consequences. Nevertheless, God already knows where we may divert from His path. He has already seen where our thoughtlessness, carelessness, and arrogance may cause us to swerve off the road and topple into the canyon of adversity.

This detour from God's chosen path may leave us feeling hopeless. How can we possibly climb back up those steep canyon walls? Who will repair the damage that has been done? Will we ever be the same? Will we ever make it to higher ground again? What do we do now?

A healing hope

When we find ourselves at the bottom of a deep pit, reflection sets in and so do our feelings of guilt and shame. Phrases like "I shouldn't have done (or said) that" parade endlessly through our minds. Beware! The enemy is keen to make us remember every insult we think we deserve *and more*! He does not want this pity party to stop. He wants us to stay in the mess and rubble of the wreck we could have avoided if we had made wiser decisions.

And to add to our remorse, Satan wants us to think that God has given up on us or that He is angry with us. I can hear it now: *You good-for-nothing, blah, blah, blah . . . Why would God even want to deal with you anymore? You did it again and made a mess of things, like you always do. What is wrong with you anyway?* I've heard it playing through my head a hundred times—a burdened, weighted head filled with shame.

Oh, how our enemy loves these moments. He relishes them. But let us not give him permission to draw them out longer than they need. It is important to know when we have done wrong and understand how we messed up, *but we do not have to stay there. God's desire is to bring us to repentance, move us into His forgiveness, and then carry us forward in newness of life.*

God is in the business of restoration. He is an expert at taking broken vessels and reworking them into something usable again. He is well known for His ability to clean up the biggest messes and bring out the greatest treasures. His forgiveness can break down prison doors and set captives free! His love can uplift the lowest soul in the depths of despair.

We may think our messes are too big to fix. We may think our missteps took us too far off His path. But our wrong turns never throw God for a loop. Remember, He has a plan, He always does. And He is inviting us to trust Him *again*—trust Him with the mess, trust Him with the cleanup plan, and trust Him with the wrongs that have been done, either by us or to us. He will take care of it all. We may have to deal with the consequences of wrong decisions, both ours and others, but we do not have to go them alone. God is on our side.

Chapter 11

The Meaning of "God With Us"

Before we jump into the rest of Joseph's story, let us take a look at how God uses difficulties in our lives. Whether we end up far from home and way off track as a result of our own choices or the choices of others, *God is still with us. He will not leave us.* If we take a detour, so does He. If we veer off a cliff, He comes with us. Wherever we end up, His Spirit pursues us.

As God's children, we have the sure and certain promise that God will never leave us nor forsake us (see Hebrews 13:5). When we go through the fire and the flood, He will be with us (Isaiah 43:1, 2). But what does His promise to be with us look like in real life when we go through trials, like Joseph's, for example? And what does God want to achieve in us and for us through His continual presence?

First of all, let us debunk a lie: Satan wants us to believe that if we do something wrong, then God will never forgive us. Satan likes to twist our thoughts so we believe that the consequences of our wrong choices are actually God's punishment. God may use the consequences to teach us important lessons but never to needlessly punish us.

But God does correct us. His correction is much like correcting an injured foot. If your foot is dislocated, not only is it painful to walk on, but it will always tend to turn your body in a certain direction. It would be very difficult to walk straight on a path if your foot were constantly trying to persuade you to go another way. Now think about this spiritually. If we are inclined to think and believe in ways that are harmful, then those negative thoughts and ideas will always tend to move us in a particular direction, like an injured foot will. So God's desire is that we work together *with Him* in the correction process. Spiritually speaking, He is inviting us to make straight paths for our feet by endeavoring to keep our eyes upon Him, thus healing our injury.

A fateful choice and a promise of restoration

Oftentimes, we want God to remove the consequences of our choices so that we do not have to deal with them. Our picture of restoration may mean pushing the reverse button or hitting delete so that we can go on like nothing happened, but that is not how it is supposed to work. Our choices will *always* have consequences, and we will *always* have to deal with them. But God wants us to know that whatever the results of our choices or others' choices may be, He is still *with* us. We see this truth so beautifully illustrated in the life of Joseph.

The whole plan of redemption reveals our Creator God's longing desire, seeking to be with us. At Creation, man and God were united in perfect harmony. Nothing separated them from each other. But Adam and Eve disobeyed God by eating from a tree He warned them not to eat from.

God values freedom of choice. So even though it was risky to give this freedom to Adam and Eve, it was God's wish that they have a choice either to follow His loving instructions or reject them. The result of choosing not to trust God has had devastating consequences for all humanity.

Adam and Eve's disobedience did not keep God from coming down to "the garden in the cool of the day" to personally be with them (Genesis 3:8). On this particular day, there was something terribly wrong. His perfect children had disregarded His warning to not eat of the tree of the knowledge of good and evil.

God called to them, but they hid and tried to cover themselves with the leaves of a plant (verse 7). Feelings of intense guilt and shame had flooded over them. They had never felt those before, causing them to do what those feelings always cause people to do—run and hide. This attempt at covering their nakedness, this hiding, marked the beginning of a process of separation between humanity and God.

Despite their fateful and faithless decision, God came to them, asking, "Where are you?" Obviously, He knew where they were and what they had done, but He *still* came to them and He *still* called to them. He gave them an opportunity to explain what had happened.

Acknowledging what they had done was important as a first step in the healing process God had come to initiate. After questioning them about what had happened, He told them, as we know all too well, that there would be serious consequences to their wrong choice. Some of the consequences were pain in childbearing for the women and the thorns and thistles that make man's work more arduous. The most notable consequence was death: "For the wages of sin is death" (Romans 6:23).

God had warned them that they would surely die if they ate of the tree of the knowledge of good and evil (Genesis 2:16, 17). Adam and Eve were created to live forever. But as a result of their disobedience, God removed them from the Garden of Eden, thus cutting off their access to the tree of life, lest sin be immortalized (Genesis 3:22–24).

The consequences of their choice were bad, really bad. These consequences would alter the course of humanity for the worse from that day forth. In spite of their inexcusable and tragic choice, God still came to be with them, and *He came with a promise.* In Genesis 3:15, God said,

> "And I will put enmity (open hostility)
> Between you [Satan] and the woman,
> And between your seed (offspring) and her Seed;
> He shall [fatally] bruise your head,
> And you shall [only] bruise His heel" (AMP).

This promise assuredly told Adam and Eve that one day, when the time was right, God would send a Savior to pay the ultimate price for their wrong choice. He loved them too much to let them die.

He loved them too much to get rid of them and start over. Instead, He would redeem them. He would restore them. He would make all things new again. And so, from that fateful day onward, He has pursued broken humanity—each and every person. And just as He came to Adam and Eve with a promise, He comes to each of us with a promise.

Healing in reconciliation

Listen to the description of Jesus, our Savior, as quoted in Matthew 1:23: " 'Behold, the virgin shall be with child, and bear a Son, and they shall call His name Immanuel,' which is translated, 'God with us.' " John 3:16 tells us that "God so loved the world that He gave His only begotten Son." The Messiah, the promised Savior, the Son of God, was not only a gift from God, but He was God coming to be Immanuel—*God with us.* He came to close the gap, remove the wedge, and reunite us to Himself.

Jesus voluntarily surrendered Himself to the weaknesses of human flesh and became like us in every way, except without sin, so that He could reunite, reconnect, and reconcile us to Himself (Philippians 2:5–8; Hebrews 2:14–17). Paul tells us that is exactly what He did; "God was in Christ reconciling the world to Himself" (2 Corinthians 5:19).

Reconciliation is the work God does in repairing the breach that has been made between Him and us. It forgives the sinner. It heals the wounds that are the inevitable consequences of our sinful choices.

God never stops pursuing us until the work of reconciliation is either completely done or completely rejected. A loving God will always run after us with open arms, no matter how far away we stray. *Wow!*

Immanuel, "God with us," means that He comes with unmerited favor, unconditional love, and unfailing forgiveness. But this is not all! If we end up in a distressing and painful situation because of someone else's heartless actions, the result of *his or her* wrong, God will help us and overrule the circumstance in ways only He can.

Again, I am reminded of the Israelites' exodus from Egypt. Right after God brought them through the Red Sea onto dry land, they began to be thirsty, but the only water available was bitter. For a long time, the Israelites had suffered a bitter life of slavery—painful, cruel, heartrending, agonizing, traumatic, and tragic. Their wounds were deep. Their identity nearly lost. Their hope nearly gone. They were thirsty for rest and remedy, and coming upon this bitter watering hole distressed them greatly.

Well, guess what? God had a plan; He always does. He told Moses to throw a particular tree into the water to make it sweet (Exodus 15:22–25). And sure enough, God's plan bought sweetness to the water so they could quench their thirst because of His loving provision.

God brought them to bitter water to show them that He alone had the ability to satisfy their needs. He wanted to show them that they could trust His remedy, guidance, and instructions because *He is the God who heals* (verse 26). Just as the Israelites needed healing, we need healing too—physical, mental, emotional, and spiritual healing.

The phrase at the end of Exodus 15:26 has great significance: "For I am the Lord who heals you." In this verse, the Hebrew word for "Lord" is *Yehovah*,[1] and the Hebrew word for "heal" is *rapha'*.[2] Thus, the name *Yehovah-Rapha* in this verse means "the Lord Who Heals." Beautiful!

In truth, "God *with* us" is "God *healing* us." He not only repairs the breach between us and forgives our sins that have separated us from Him (Isaiah 59:1, 2, 16), but He also heals our brokenness—the damage caused by our sins and the wounds that have been inflicted upon us.

As God promises to be with us, His plan is to heal us. Jesus is the One

> Who forgives all your iniquities,
> Who heals all your diseases,
> Who redeems your life from destruction,
> Who crowns you with lovingkindness and tender mercies,

Who satisfies your mouth with good things,
So that your youth is renewed like the eagle's (Psalm 103:3–5).

He heals the brokenhearted
And binds up their wounds (Psalm 147:3).

"For I will restore health to you
And heal you of your wounds," says the Lord (Jeremiah 30:17).

When Jesus walked upon this earth, He brought healing and restoration wherever He went. The miracles He performed confirmed that He was the promised Messiah—*the Anointed One*—whose mission as Immanuel was

"to preach good tidings to the poor; . . .
. . . to heal the brokenhearted,
To proclaim liberty to the captives,
And the opening of the prison to those who are bound; . . .
To comfort all who mourn, . . .
To give them beauty for ashes,
The oil of joy for mourning,
The garment of praise for the spirit of heaviness" (Isaiah 61:1–3).

So it is that God comes to be with us as our Savior, and He comes with the promise of forgiveness, reconciliation, restoration, and healing.

Now we are ready to dig back into Joseph's story.

---

1. Strong's Hebrew Lexicon (NKJV), s.v. "H3068–*Yehovah*," Blue Letter Bible, accessed January 25, 2021, https://www.blueletterbible.org/lang/lexicon/lexicon.cfm?Strongs=H3068&t=NKJV.

2. Strong's Hebrew Lexicon (NKJV), s.v. "H7495–*rapha'*," Blue Letter Bible, accessed January 25, 2021, https://www.blueletterbible.org/lang/lexicon/lexicon.cfm?Strongs=H7495&t=NKJV.

Chapter 12

A Surprising Time to Thrive

At first glance, Joseph's situation as a slave in Egypt appeared bleak. The Ishmaelites had brought Joseph to Egypt and sold him to a man named Potiphar. Nevertheless, God planned to be with Joseph and also prosper him. "The Lord was with Joseph, and he was a successful man. . . . And his master saw that the Lord was with him and that the Lord made all he did to prosper in his hand" (Genesis 39:2, 3).

Where was his prosperity as a slave? God's idea of prosperity does not always look the way we think it will. Being successful in God's eyes rarely means the accumulation of things or fame. Success in the truest sense really means being victorious and triumphing over the various challenges and temptations we face (especially if we are in a hard situation already). In Joseph's situation, *prosperity* meant thriving and flourishing, regardless of his circumstances.

Oftentimes, the first thing we think when we are in a bad situation is, *This is horrible! There is nothing good about this. The whole thing is awful!* We tend to see only tragedy with no potential for good—all gloom and glum. But even though we have ended up in a horrible place, God has a plan to prosper us if we choose to remain faithful to Him. Listen to God's words in Jeremiah 29:11: "For I know the thoughts that I think toward you, says the Lord, thoughts of peace and not of evil, to give you a future and a hope."

Even though God sometimes allows bad things to happen to us, and even though He sometimes leads us through troubling circumstances, He does not think, plan, or cause evil for us. It is His plan, regardless of the circumstances, to help us overcome difficulties, endure hardships, and grow in our relationship with Him as we place our trust in Him.

Success means overcoming difficulties and struggles through God's power. In the context of being in a horrible place or situation (for example, being a slave in Egypt), success can mean gaining the strength and courage to do the best we can under the circumstances. It can mean putting one foot in front of the other, taking one step at a time, and moving forward—just like Joseph did.

To me, *flounder* is a word that contrasts greatly with *prosper*. "To flounder" is to try to stay afloat without knowing how to swim. We thrash around, making a whole lot of splashing and commotion, without making any progress. It is exhausting. It wears us out, and soon, without a change of action, the water will overtake us and we will drown. Joseph could have easily floundered in his situation. He was out of his element, out of his comfort zone, and in way over his head. Nevertheless, the Lord's plan was to take His wounded boy and prosper him *where he was*. Joseph was keen to grab hold of God and rely upon Him for survival, and *prosperity is found in that choice.*

Joseph had been adored by his father. It is likely that the lifestyle his father created for him gave Joseph an attitude of self-sufficiency and arrogance—character traits that are very difficult to overcome at any time but especially later in life.

At first glance, the suffering at the hands of his brothers seemed like the worst thing that could happen to Joseph, but it brought about a change in his heart and character that prepared him for his new life in Egypt and its many challenges. That is not to say that what happened to him was good. No, but good came out of it. We can look at a bad situation and think that nothing good can ever come out of it, but God promises, "And we know that all things work together for good to those who love God, to those who are the called according to His purpose" (Romans 8:28).

How many things work together for good? *Everything!*

Joseph chose to put his trust in God and serve Him with *all* of his heart, and God made Joseph successful in *all* he did. Even though we may find ourselves far from the path we planned, God is there to help us stand back up and start putting one foot in front of the other. "Keep walking," He whispers, "I'm here to help you."

This detour can feel like falling off a cliff. We may have to meander aimlessly on the low valley floor for a while. We may have to deal with new challenges. We may be out of our comfort zones and in over our heads, but God will help us succeed. As we walk forward, trusting Him and leaning upon Him, He will bring us success. Like Joseph, our success may be in the little things at first. Do not believe for one second that God wants to punish us. No! He wants to make us successful *where we are* as we move forward with faith in Him.

Chapter 13

In the Dungeon

Potiphar, the captain of Pharaoh's guard, was very pleased with Joseph, so much so that he put Joseph in charge of everything he had. And "the Lord blessed the Egyptian's house for Joseph's sake; and the blessing of the Lord was on all that he had in the house and in the field" (Genesis 39:5).

Then "his master's wife cast longing eyes on Joseph, and she said, 'Lie with me' " (verse 7). Joseph refused to sin against his God and refused to betray his master's trust. This, however, did not stop Potiphar's wife in her seductive schemes. "She spoke to Joseph day by day," but he would not listen to her or give in to her desires (verse 10). So one day she grabbed his clothing, and in an effort to avoid her, Joseph ran from her, leaving his garment in her hands. Potiphar's wife avenged herself by accusing him of attempted assault. This account is recorded in Genesis 39:16–20:

> So she kept his garment with her until his master came home. Then she spoke to him with words like these, saying, "The Hebrew servant whom you brought to us came in to me to mock me; so it happened, as I lifted my voice and cried out, that he left his garment with me and fled outside."
>
> So it was, when his master heard the words which his wife spoke to him, saying, "Your servant did to me after this manner," that his anger was aroused. Then Joseph's master took him and put him into the prison, a place where the king's prisoners were

confined. And he was there in the prison.

What happened to Joseph as a result of Mrs. Potiphar's accusation? He was cast into prison. How unfair! Joseph did not do anything wrong. In fact, he was trying to be an upright, honest man, and yet great trouble still came his way! Where was God when this happened? Again Genesis records, "But the LORD was with Joseph and showed him mercy, and He gave him favor in the sight of the keeper of the prison" (Genesis 39:21).

When we could say that all was lost—Joseph was surely forsaken then—God never left him. Under these extremely trying circumstances, it must have been difficult for Joseph to understand God's mercy, and yet this verse specifically mentions that God "showed him mercy."

We need to be careful what we believe "mercy" would look like, because to us, "mercy" might be interpreted as immediate deliverance from prison and everything turning out well. At first, we may not recognize God's mercy because it does not bring about the grand deliverance we may be looking for. But oftentimes, it is God's will to keep us in difficult circumstances and bless us while we are in the "dungeon" because He has a plan for us there. *Within God's plan, as we look to Him for direction, He shows us opportunities disguised as obstacles that unwrap His gifts of mercy.*

We read in Genesis 39:22, 23, "And the keeper of the prison committed to Joseph's hand all the prisoners who were in the prison; whatever they did there, it was his doing. The keeper of the prison did not look into anything that was under Joseph's authority, because the LORD was with him; and whatever he did, the LORD made it prosper." God's mercy was opening up the favor of the prison guard to Joseph, and he put him to work by entrusting him with everything. Joseph did not have to accept to this responsibility; he could have chosen to wallow in self-pity. Thankfully, he did not.

Naturally, when in a situation like Joseph's, we can often be tempted to dwell solely upon ourselves and our misfortune. There would have been plenty of time for Joseph to mull over the unfairness of his situation. There was certainly plenty of injustice to think about and a whole slew of accusations he could have voiced. Joseph could have easily allowed himself to become an enraged and bitter prisoner.

The power of God's love
It is so easy to think repeatedly of the brash, inconsiderate, and selfish actions of others that have inflicted such pain and discomfort upon us. Satan loves it when our minds are darkened by these painful reflections. He tries to influence us to play them over and over again in our heads, constantly rerunning them, digging deeper, and keeping the wounds open and aching.

Such reiterations of the tragedies we have experienced and the injustices we have suffered cripple and enslave us. They beat us down again and again. They constantly excite our anger and the desire for revenge. Quickly, roots of bitterness and resentment begin to work their way into every aspect of our lives. These roots of bitterness begin to cover every outlook and cloud every thought; they dampen every hope and still every joy. Depression locks in and settles deep. We fall ever downward into the enemy's land of war—one that is full of spiritual land mines.

God does not want us to live embittered, angry, hurt, and emotionally crippled lives, but that is where the enemy is constantly trying to lead us. There have been many times when my focus was locked into this merry-go-round of wrongs that someone committed against me. Resentment, bitterness, and pain enslaved me and threatened to drive me far from the peace, love, and joy found in Jesus.

I am reminded of a time when Jesus came to the temple to teach, as He often did. Early one morning as people were gathered around Jesus, listening to Him speak, they were disrupted by a great commotion. A group of Pharisees dragged a terror-stricken woman before the crowd and threw her at Jesus' feet. "Teacher, this woman was caught in adultery, in the very act" (John 8:4). They pointed at her with scowling contempt. "Now Moses, in the law, commanded us that such should be stoned. But what do You say?" (verse 5).

They looked to Jesus with gleeful anticipation, urging Him to confront the issue head-on. Secretly, they had hoped to ensnare Jesus and find fault with His judgment so they could have reason to arrest Him. But Jesus quickly discerned their evil intent. He was not caught up in their heartless fury. He directed His eyes to the trembling woman.

This woman had done wrong, clearly; she had committed adultery. But this high-minded group of scowling religious leaders had set her up and were using her to find fault with Jesus. Her fate was in His hands. What would He do?

They had hoped He would either denounce Moses' law by excusing the woman or condemn the woman to death according to Moses' law. To do either one would have been sufficient cause to convict Him. If He excused the woman, they would be able to convict Him of despising Moses' law and authority. If He condemned the woman to death according to Moses' law, He would violate Roman rule, which alone claimed the authority to inflict the death penalty.

Jesus knew Moses' law concerning the affair at hand, and He recognized how the Pharisees were wrong in their current application of the law. It specifically applied to a domestic dispute in which a husband accused his wife of adultery. In such a case, the husband *had* to have witnesses. Then both parties involved would be punished equally.

Without a word, "Jesus stooped down and wrote on the ground with His finger" (verse 6). The Pharisees were annoyed with Jesus' delay in pronouncing judgment, so they kept asking Him what He would do.

He stood up and said simply, "He who is without sin among you, let him throw a stone at her first" (verse 7). Surprised at His words, the Pharisees stopped and watched Him as He stooped down and again began writing in the dirt. The words He wrote convicted them of their own sins, and one by one, they shuffled away ashamed.

After they had left, Jesus stood back up and looked at their intended victim. "Woman," He said in the kindest tones, "where are those accusers of yours? Has no one condemned you?" (verse 10).

"No one, Lord," she responded in a quivering voice.

With both solemnity and joy, Jesus revealed His mercy and love for the afflicted. "Neither do I condemn you; go and sin no more," He said to her (verse 11). Here it is fitting to remember the famous passage in John 3:17: "For God did not send His Son into the world to condemn the world, but that the world through Him might be saved." Did God send Jesus to Earth to condemn us? *No!*

The healing power of God's forgiveness

Why did Jesus come? Jesus came to save us from bondage. That means bondage from the past and the present. Like the woman in John 8, Joseph also had to learn the lesson of giving and receiving forgiveness. Unless we, like Joseph and the woman in John 8, learn how to give and receive forgiveness, we will be weighed down under the burden and stain of someone else's crime upon us. Where our abuser stands over us with condemnation and mockery, our Savior invites us to take His hand of forgiveness, mercy, and love. Jesus wants to lift us up from the ground where we have been thrown and set us upon the rock of His salvation (Psalm 40:2).

I encourage you today to accept God's guidance and trust His provision—His promises of forgiveness, restoration, grace, and healing set us free from the past, our own sins, and the horrible crimes others may have done to us.

It is important to note that God does not condone other people's crimes when He brings healing into our lives. His work of grace does not disregard or excuse what they have done, and it does not overlook the pain they have inflicted. It removes us from the house of bitterness; it dislodges us from a vengeful battleground by placing the criminal in God's hands.

In Deuteronomy 32:35, God says,

> "Vengeance is Mine, and recompense;
> Their foot shall slip in due time;
> For the day of their calamity is at hand,
> And the things to come hasten upon them."

In other words, there are consequences that people who have perpetrated evil will have to deal with as a result of the wrongs they have inflicted on others. What those consequences are, we may never know, but God, in His infinite wisdom and justice, will deal with evildoers.

This is not to say that we should not bring offenders to face legal consequences, if possible (Romans 13:3, 4). Sometimes the laws of the land provide means for conviction and justice. Regretfully, there are times in which victims of cruelty are silenced and never granted the ability to pursue justice. Not everyone who commits a crime is found out or brought to justice. God desires to bring healing into our lives while also dealing with the abuser with divine wisdom that is beyond our insight and knowledge.

With God's healing comes a sweet, cleansing surge of forgiveness into our hearts. It comes from *His heart* to *our hearts*. Forgiveness is meant to wash away all of our guilt and shame and purge us of the need to bear our sins. We can leave our sins at Jesus' feet. Forgiveness happens when Jesus shows us that all of our accusers have been silenced by His hand of authority and voice of wisdom. We can look up and see His face of tenderness and pity. His hand of grace is already there to lift us up. "I do not condemn you," He tells us.

Gradually, His forgiveness permeates our entire lives, if we desire it to. It will go where we had never thought it could. It will extend to others, even to those who have wronged us. And the freedom and exhilarating joy of being released from the bondage of bitterness and hatred are beyond the most beautiful words I can write. Forgiveness is simply a miracle.

Forgiveness does not whitewash the wrongs that have been done to us, and it does not excuse those wrongs in God's eyes. Those who have wronged us must reckon with God themselves. The battle is between God and them, not us and them anymore. We can walk away and leave them in God's hands—in His justice, His judgment, and His reckoning. Forgiveness frees us from spending our time and energy focusing on the wrongs committed against us and those who committed them, releasing the mental choke holds we have on each other. Accepting God's forgiveness and freely offering forgiveness to those who have wronged us will remove the bitterness from our hearts and allow us to grow into disciples whom God can use in unique situations He has prepared us for—just like Joseph.

In a sense, those who have wronged us become like old stones that we have carried for too long. God invites us to release them into His hands. Symbolically, this is like dropping stones into the ocean and watching them disappear into the depths. There is nothing we can do about them anymore; they are gone and are out of our hands. Only God knows where they went and what to do with them. They are no longer ours to worry about. We do not possess these "stones" anymore. They do not weigh us down anymore. We have let them go. God invites us to continue to walk in His peace, freedom, and healing.

Stepping into freedom through God
At some point, Joseph accepted the freedom that comes when we accept God's forgiveness and extend it to those who have wronged us. Psalm 37 describes it in these wonderful steps:

1. "Do not fret because of evildoers" (verse 1).
2. "Trust in the Lord, and do good" (verse 3).
3. "Delight yourself also in the Lord" (verse 4).
4. "Commit your way to the Lord" (verse 5).
5. "Rest in the Lord, and wait patiently for Him" (verse 7).
6. "Cease from anger, and forsake wrath" (verse 8).

In one sense, our anger at abuse can be appropriate. Who would not be angry over evil, especially committed against the innocent? Who would not be angry at brothers who betrayed and sold us into slavery? But at the same time, our anger does not lead us to peace. It acts as a tyrant over us, constantly arousing indignation and behaving like a troubled sea in which there is no rest. Where we might think that our anger is justified, the Bible warns us that "the wrath of man does not produce the righteousness of God" (James 1:20). This is a warning to not go where only God can and should go; only God can deal with the offenders and the abusers in a way that is right.

God will fight for us; He will go to war for us. "For the LORD your God is He who goes with you, to fight for you" (Deuteronomy 20:4; see also Exodus 14:14). It is really hard to put into someone else's hand something that we are passionate about. But when we put something in God's hands, we can know that it is in the *best* of hands!

Furthermore, our anger provokes the desire for revenge, which is a type of maliciousness that only goes in the wrong direction at an ever-escalating pace. When we release our anger and desire for vengeance into God's capable hands, a flood of peace, rest, and freedom comes into our lives. We are no longer held captive to the claims of vengeance or are victims of relentless rage.

Someone might ask, "Well, what about the kind of anger that swirls up like a tornado to protect ourselves or a loved one from harm?" Let me share some wisdom from Ecclesiastes:

> To everything there is a season,
> A time for every purpose under heaven: . . .
> A time to kill,
> And a time to heal; . . .
> A time to keep silence,
> And a time to speak;
> A time to love,
> And a time to hate;
> A time of war,
> And a time of peace (Ecclesiastes 3:1, 3, 7, 8).

There is a time to rise up and defend and a time to walk away and be silent. There is a proper time and season to act a certain way in every circumstance, and if we are willing to listen, the Holy Spirit will reveal to us when and how to act. This was a lesson Joseph learned deeply.

Let us reflect on a time when David had to deal with a situation where it was best for him to act a certain way in the face of danger. King Saul knew that the Lord was with David. Therefore, he feared that the kingdom would be given to David. This troubled Saul greatly. He grew increasingly jealous of David. One day, while David was playing the harp, Saul picked up a spear and said to himself, "I will pin David to the wall!" (1 Samuel 18:11).

The first counsel for David that comes to mind may well be: *Stand your ground and fight back, David! After all, God has already anointed you as the next king. Saul has instigated the attack, so you have the right to fight back.* Well, that is not what David did. He ran away. What kind of a man runs away? Can you imagine the ridicule? "Look at him run away! He is a loser, a coward, and a good-for-nothing wimp!" Yet the Bible tells us that in *this* situation, "David behaved wisely in all his ways, and the Lord was with him" (verse 14). It was not time for David to fight. He was wise to run away.

This world has its way of dealing with issues, and often it involves all manner of fighting, biting, kicking, yelling, hitting, pushing, and "spear throwing." Many of us have grown up with this type of example, and we may have engaged in one or more of those behaviors ourselves. Of course, if we did not fight and stand our ground, then there was a clamor of voices, telling us that we were weak, pathetic losers. And who wants to be ridiculed and taunted?

David fled the scene, not because he could not have fought and won, not because he was a coward, but because it was not time for him to fight. If God was going to give him the kingdom, David would wait for God's timing. God gave David discernment on how to act and what to do in his situation, and I know that He will guide us too. In every circumstance, we need to pray and seek the Lord to understand how we are to react.

As in Joseph's case, he could have chosen to let the "root of bitterness" spring up in him and worsen his already miserable circumstances (Hebrews 12:15). Despite the temptation to fall into the depths of resentment, Joseph chose to walk into the mercy-filled opportunities God was setting before him while in prison.

It was God's plan to use Joseph in a meaningful and rewarding ministry. While idleness and depression could have prevailed for Joseph, God instead provided a purpose and a mission. How often do we look for opportunities to minister to others who are right *where we are?* How often do we uplift and encourage others who are bound in the same adverse circumstances and imprisoned in trials similar to our own? Such a work would brighten our nights and put a song in our hearts. God has designed that by uplifting others, we will be lifted up ourselves.

Although prison was not where Joseph wanted to be, he discerned that God's immediate plan for him was to look beyond himself and engage in a meaningful and purposeful work. In prison, Joseph could give encouragement and care for other inmates. Prison was a place where he could learn to cultivate compassion and empathy for others. There he could and would learn how to best minister to other people with wisdom and pity. And because he chose God's plan for him in that unpleasant place, "whatever he did, the Lord made it prosper" (Genesis 39:23).

Chapter 14

Forgotten and Forlorn

After Joseph had been in prison for a while, there was a problem with Pharaoh's personal butler and baker. Somehow they had offended him so much that he threw them both into prison, and the captain of the guard put Joseph in charge of them (Genesis 40:3, 4).

Then the butler and the baker each had a troubling dream on the same night (verse 5). In the morning, when Joseph checked on them, he noticed they were more despondent than usual. "Why do you look so sad today?" Joseph asked them (verse 7).

They told him, "We each have had a dream, and there is no interpreter of it" (verse 8).

"Do not interpretations belong to God?" Joseph asked them. "Tell them to me, please" (verse 8). So they told Joseph their dreams. Joseph told them the interpretations to their dreams. The butler would be restored to the king's favor and be the chief butler again, but the baker would be hung. According to the dreams, all of this was to be fulfilled in three days.

Seeing an opportunity, Joseph asked the butler to remember him and show him kindness by asking Pharaoh to let him out of jail. "For indeed I was stolen away from the land of the Hebrews," he said, "and also I have done nothing here that they should put me into the dungeon" (verse 15).

Joseph's interpretation was fulfilled exactly three days later; it was Pharaoh's birthday, and he restored the butler to his position, but the baker was hung. Everything happened just as God had revealed to Joseph in the interpretation of the dreams. There was just one problem. The chief butler "did not remember" his promise to Joseph "but forgot him" (verse 23).

Just as Joseph was forgotten, the truth is that many times people will forget their promises to us. Not only can we be treated unfairly, conspired against, and cut off by our own families, but we can also be forgotten by people who have promised to remember us! At times, we may be stood up, left high and dry, stranded, and abandoned. People may turn their backs on us and pretend they never knew us. They may even walk out on us and leave us without a parting word.

It is painful to feel a lack of care, concern, and appreciation; it is also painful to feel a sense of rejection. Many people feel alone, overlooked, ignored, disregarded, and unrecognized. Their plight is shrugged off, their desperate circumstances are not taken into account, and their struggles are met with indifference.

Forgotten but not alone

During Jesus' darkest hour and the most intense trial of His life, His closest friends abandoned Him (Mark 14:50). One of them, Judas, sold Him for a few coins and led the soldiers to arrest Him, betraying Him with a kiss (Matthew 26:15, 47–56). Jesus' friends had promised to stay by His side, no matter what would happen. But when the time came to prove their promise, they deserted Him (verses 35, 56).

Furthermore, after running away, Peter came back to see what was happening to Jesus. People could not help but notice that Peter had been seen with Jesus and how he sounded like a Galilean—just like the other disciples did. When questioned whether he knew Jesus or was one of Jesus' friends, he denied everything. Three times Peter denied having any connection with Jesus (Mark 14:66–72).

After being denied and abandoned, Jesus faced mockings, beatings, false accusations, and angry mobs, with no consoling human friend by His side.

Before this, multitudes had sought Jesus, bringing their sick and dying to benefit from His healing touch; now many abandoned

Him. They had gathered in great throngs to hear His words and had sat by His feet in awe of His teachings. They had joyfully received His miracles. Jesus had been favored as an honored guest at feasts and in private homes alike, but now the previously desired One, the honored One, the sought-after One, became the unwanted One. The Master of love had become unloved. No one wanted to associate with this condemned Man. Very few seemed to understand His mission and mercy. Very few seemed to discern the significance of His sacrifice, test, and trial. He was making the greatest sacrifice of love this world has ever known, and no one seemed to appreciate it.

And in His darkest hour, lifted up for all to see, Jesus felt completely alone. Would His sacrifice be enough to reconcile fallen humanity to infinite Holiness? Who could fathom the anguish of His soul and the lonely trial that He alone had to endure? Prophetic words in Psalm 69:20 reveal His distress:

Reproach has broken my heart,
And I am full of heaviness;
I looked for someone to take pity, but there was none;
And for comforters, but I found none.

The intense enormity of guilt pressed on Jesus as He took the sinner's place upon the cross. Jesus knew and understood the Father's great abhorrence for evil and sin, but now He felt the vast chasm between Himself and Almighty God, for "He made Christ who knew no sin to [judicially] be sin on our behalf" (2 Corinthians 5:21, AMP). And at that moment, Jesus felt as if the enduring strength of His Father's constant presence was being wholly withdrawn from Him. In deep anguish of soul and amazement, He cried out to His Father, "My God, My God, why have You forsaken Me?" (Matthew 27:46). He was truly forsaken of men, and He *felt* truly forsaken of God.

Luke 23:44 tells us that "about the sixth hour, . . . there was darkness over all the earth until the ninth hour." So from about noon until three in the afternoon, an unnatural, thick darkness covered the land. In this darkness that fell on the scene, I believe that God drew very near to His dying Son. Psalm 18:11 tells us that "He made darkness His secret place; His canopy around Him was dark waters and thick clouds of the skies." The darkness in this verse is obviously talking about a literal darkness that acts as a covering or veil. God made darkness to be like a pavilion (*cukkah* in Hebrew[1]) or tent that obscured His presence. It hid Him from sight.

Jesus felt the separation that sin causes between the sinful and the holy, the death bound and the Life-Giver, and in that moment, He felt utterly forsaken by His Father. He had never felt the loss of His Father's presence before. They had always been intrinsically connected in perfect harmony until this moment of darkness when God hid His face from His Son as He became sin (Isaiah 59:1, 2). "Clouds and darkness surround Him; righteousness and justice are the foundation of His throne" (Psalm 97:2). Jesus could not discern the presence of His Father or the holy angels at the side of His cross.

Jesus, our Savior, knows what it is like to be overlooked, unappreciated, and misunderstood. He knows what it is like to feel unwanted and uncared for. He knows what it is like to feel loneliness and utter isolation. He knows what it is like to be betrayed and abandoned by friends.

Even though Jesus *felt* forsaken by His Father, He was not. And Jesus will not forsake us or let us down. He does not treat us as we treat each other. We may seem to be wholly alone and our situation disregarded, but Jesus has seen. We may feel completely abandoned and neglected, but God has considered us. We may feel as though no one cares about our suffering or how unfairly we have been treated, but God knows. Hagar, whom we learned about earlier, felt alone and devalued, but she discovered that God saw her plight and cared about her, for He is El Roi, the *God who sees us*!

Value in the eyes of God

In Matthew 13:44–46, Jesus tells us two parables:

"The kingdom of heaven is like treasure hidden in a field, which a man found and hid; and for joy over it he goes and sells all that he has and buys that field.

"Again, the kingdom of heaven is like a merchant seeking beautiful pearls, who, when he had found one pearl of great price, went and sold all that he had and bought it."

The first parable describes a man finding a hidden treasure and his willingness to sell everything in order to obtain that treasure, which is the kingdom of heaven. The second parable describes the kingdom of heaven as a merchant. In 1 Corinthians 6:20, we are told, "For you were bought at a price; therefore glorify God in your body and in your spirit, which are God's." Jesus is the Merchant, seeking fine pearls for which He is willing to pay a great price. His death was certainly a high price to pay—the highest price one could pay for anything. It reveals that our Savior sees humanity as a treasure that He would give up everything for. We are of infinite worth to Him. That being said, we can be absolutely sure that He will never forget us or abandon us.

Centuries earlier, Joseph was forgotten by those who said they would remember him, but he was not forgotten by God. We can be assured that even though others may consider us unworthy, God considers us of great value.

Satan likes for us to believe that if we are forsaken by men, then we must also be forsaken by God. He wants us to value ourselves according to the value others place on us, so then, when people treat us badly or abandon us, we tend to think we are worthless. The next logical step is to ask, If other people do not seem to value us, then why should God?

The truth is that God's love for and esteem of us were demonstrated abundantly when He sent His only Son to save us. Our Savior's love was revealed in His selfless life as He constantly went about ministering to the needs of humanity. Jesus' love was confirmed when He demonstrated that He was willing not only to give up everything for us but also His very life. As the Merchant, He showed us that He places great value on us—as does all of heaven. We are worth everything to Him. Friends and strangers alike may think very little of us at some point in our lives, but our Savior thinks very highly of us and *always will*. To Him, we are precious pearls. Just listen to these words in Zephaniah 3:17:

> "The LORD your God in your midst,
> The Mighty One, will save;
> He will rejoice over you with gladness,
> He will quiet you with His love,
> He will rejoice over you with singing."

And the wonderful thing is that we can know that we will never fall out of His love. Because "Jesus Christ is the same yesterday, today, and forever" (Hebrews 13:8).

---

1. Strong's Hebrew Lexicon (NKJV), s.v. "H5521–*cukkah*," Blue Letter Bible, accessed January 26, 2021, https://www.blueletterbible.org/lang/lexicon/lexicon.cfm?Strongs=H5521&t=NKJV.

Chapter 15

Wait on the Lord

The Bible tells us that Joseph was forgotten by the butler for two full years. That is a long time to remain in jail for something he did not do! I can imagine him wondering, *Will I ever get out of here?*

Two years later Pharaoh had two dreams, and when he woke up, "his spirit was troubled" (Genesis 41:8). He called for all the magicians and all the wise men of Egypt to interpret the dreams, but no one could help. Then the butler remembered Joseph.

The butler relayed to Pharaoh how he and the baker had dreamed dreams while in prison. "There was a young Hebrew man with us there, a servant of the captain of the guard. And we told him, and he interpreted our dreams for us. . . . And it came to pass, just as he interpreted for us, so it happened" (verses 12, 13).

So Pharaoh called for Joseph, and they quickly brought him out of the dungeon. Pharaoh said to Joseph, "I have had a dream, and there is no one who can interpret it. But I have heard it said of you that you can understand a dream, to interpret it" (verse 15).

Joseph answered Pharaoh, saying, "It is not in me; God will give Pharaoh an answer of peace" (verse 16). So Pharaoh told Joseph the dreams, and Joseph interpreted them for him. "The dreams of Pharaoh are one; God has shown Pharaoh what He is about to do" (verse 25). There would be seven years of plenty followed by seven years of severe famine. Since God had given the same type of dream to Pharaoh twice, it meant that the times ahead were prepared by God, and these events would happen very soon (verse 32).

The interpretation came with instructions on how to best prepare for the coming crisis. Joseph proceeded to tell Pharaoh that he needed a wise and vigilant man to oversee the preparations for the coming crisis. Pharaoh needed to appoint officers over the land who were responsible for making sure one-fifth of Egypt's bounty was collected for seven years. In the cities, corn was to be stored up for the tough times ahead, so "that the land may not perish during the famine" (verse 36).

The interpretation and instruction sounded good to Pharaoh and all of his servants. So they set about looking for an overseer for the grain-collection project. "Can we find such a one as this, a man in whom is the Spirit of God?" Pharaoh said, pointing to Joseph. "Inasmuch as God has shown you all this, there is no one as discerning and wise as you. You shall be over my house, and all my people shall be ruled according to your word; only in regard to the throne will I be greater than you" (verses 38–40). Pharaoh took his ring from his hand and put it on Joseph's hand and had him dressed in fine clothes and put a gold chain around his neck.

What an incredible change of events! What might have gone through Joseph's mind in response to all this? Who could have imagined what God had planned for Joseph?

More than a decade had passed from the time Joseph had his own dreams until the time he stood in the king's court. God was maneuvering Joseph into an important position in Egypt so He could continue to prosper His people. During the time of famine, Joseph's brothers would come to Egypt seeking corn, and when they came, Joseph would be God's chosen man to be in the right place at the right time. He had been appointed for a specific purpose. He had been chosen for a specific time. But he had to wait on God's timing and wisdom.

He was seventeen when he was sold by his brothers into slavery and thirty when Pharaoh made him ruler over all of his house (verse 46). During those years, he had been unfairly mistreated, falsely accused, and conspired against more than once, and now here he stood. He had finally been lifted out of slavery and out of the dungeon into the king's palace, with the king's ring upon his finger and with kingly robes upon his shoulders. Looking back, it was clear everything had been perfectly ordained by God. Even though some did not act according to God's will, God's plan was still accomplished to the letter—just as Joseph's dreams had foretold.

Waiting on God brought Joseph to the place where God wanted him. Obviously, God had some things to work out before Joseph could be put into position. Part of the preparation included molding Joseph into a man able to rule the land of Egypt with wisdom and humility. To prepare Joseph, God delayed his release from prison.

Have you ever been held up in traffic or been delayed in getting out the door because something unexpected came up? Later you found out that there had been a devastating accident or disaster on the very road where you were headed, and you would definitely have been involved in that accident if you had not been late. It is no surprise that God was working on your behalf, and that meant delaying you from rushing off into a terrible situation that might have even killed you. God's timing is perfect, even though He may not be working exactly according to our schedules, desires, or understanding.

I have often wondered about the people who were caught up in a devastating accident that we escaped. We feel so fortunate and blessed. But what about them? What about the people who were not "so lucky"? For one thing, we do not know all the details. God is working in everyone's lives to some extent or another, depending on how much they are responding to His Spirit. Perhaps they ignored and disregarded the promptings of His voice of wisdom. Perhaps God's plan led them into the accident, like He led Daniel into the lions' den and David through "the valley of the shadow of death" (Psalm 23:4).

We do not know all the details, but there will come a time when God will show us everything. From the portals of heaven, we will see unseen hands working on our behalf throughout our entire lives. And "at the name of Jesus every knee should bow, . . . and that every tongue should confess," in acknowledgment and reverence, "that Jesus Christ is Lord" (Philippians 2:10, 11; see also Romans 14:11, 12). Until the time when we will see how and why everything was the way it was, we must simply "walk by faith, not by sight" (2 Corinthians 5:7).

Lessons on waiting

If anyone in the Bible learned to wait on the Lord, that person was David. Let us review a bit of his story. God's people, the children of Israel, wanted a king. God appointed Saul to be their king. Saul had been put in a highly responsible position by God. His responsibility was great. But there came a time when he no longer listened to God's wisdom and promptings. In his arrogance, he made a series of terrible mistakes that cost the lives of many people. Eventually, God decided enough was enough and Saul was no longer worthy to be king over His people.

Though God had rejected Saul as a king, I believe that He had not given up on him as an individual. Many times we read in the biblical account that God sent Saul a troubling spirit (1 Samuel 18:10). Have you ever been troubled by something you did that was wrong? Has your conscience ever been troubled by a strong conviction? God sends us strong convictions when we have done something wrong. Their purpose is not to hit us over the head but bring us to confession and repentance. From there, God wants to move us forward to forgiveness, peace, healing, and restoration.

God consistently pursued Saul with that troubling spirit, but he would not listen. When we fight conviction, we may, tragically and sadly, become hardened and unwilling to hear the voice of God.

While Saul was still king, God told the prophet Samuel to go and anoint another king. David was just a young shepherd at the time, perhaps around fifteen years old, yet Samuel anointed him king! He was thirty years old when he was finally able to rule as king of Judah, and it was another seven years before he became king of Israel too (2 Samuel 5:1–5).

In the waiting time, between the anointing and the appointing, David was treated unfairly by Saul and conspired against more than once. There was hardly a time when he could lay down his head in peace. He was almost always running for his life, dwelling in caves, in the wilderness, and in enemy territory. The time between his anointing and appointing can be summed up in two words: *time* and *trouble*.

Certainly, there was a reason God did not make David king sooner. He knew that this young man was not yet ready to be king. David had a lot to learn before he could competently and wisely rule over God's people. David was not a perfect man, but he was willing to trust that God's timing was best. Because of that and more, God called David "a man after My own heart" (Acts 13:22).

When it comes to difficult times, we often set a timer on God: *If this is not over within five minutes, I'm out of here! Ding! Time's up, God.* Sometimes we feel quite dejected because, to all appearances, He did not listen to us. It seems like He let us down. And we have walked ourselves right into the place where Satan was luring us: *God does not care about me because if He really cared for and loved me, He would not have let this problem happen to me, and He would have been here by now, making everything right!* And bam, we just jumped off Satan's cliff of doubt.

In the Bible, we are instructed and reminded repeatedly to "wait on the LORD." Many of those verses are found in the Psalms as David expressed his need and his desire while waiting on God's initiatives. In Psalm 27:14, he wrote,

> Wait on the LORD;
> Be of good courage,
> And He shall strengthen your heart;
> Wait, I say, on the LORD!

Why does it take courage to wait on God? Remember Noah! God told him to build an ark—a really big boat. He lived in a time when "the earth was filled with violence" (Genesis 6:11). Everyone "had corrupted their way on the earth" (verse 12). So much so "that every intent of the thoughts of [man's] . . . heart was only evil continually" (verse 5). That means day and night, without a break, nonstop evil.

God was going to send a flood to cleanse the earth (verse 17). Whoever believed Noah's message of warning and his call to repentance from their evil ways would be saved. Mercifully, there would be ample room in the boat for everyone. During that time, it seems as if Noah was a totally ineffective preacher. One hundred and twenty years passed as he built the boat and preached about the coming flood, and the only ones who believed him enough to jump on board before the rain began were his seven family members (Matthew 24:37–39; Genesis 7:7).

Facing unbelief, corruption, violence, and mockery on every side, Noah could have easily given up. No one believed him until it started to rain, and by then, it was too late. It took courage to continue to preach the warning message and build God's lifeboat. It took strength to continue extending the invitation to get on board. It took nerve to continue working on the same project for one hundred and twenty years without persuading many people to believe. We need to follow Noah's example: No matter what people are telling you, keep trusting God. He is still working on your behalf. He still has a wonderful plan for your life. Sometimes your faith may look ill advised until, like Noah, it starts to rain. Stay strong, and your faith will be rewarded.

Working while waiting

Noah waited for a long time before God sent the promised floodwaters, but he definitely was not sitting idly by during that time. He had been commissioned by God to build a boat and preach a message. Moving forward, day by day, wooden plank by wooden plank, Noah worked for God and with God.

What about Joseph in the dungeon? God had put Joseph to work, taking care of prisoners. While Joseph waited for God to solve his problem, he did not sit idle either. And that is a very important lesson for us today. God always has a meaningful and purposeful work for us to do wherever we are as we patiently wait on the Lord. Waiting on God does not mean being idle.

Just after the children of Israel had been freed from slavery, the Egyptians came running after them to capture them again. And as they were bearing down on the Israelites, Moses said to the people, "Do not be afraid. Stand still, and see the salvation of the LORD, which He will accomplish for you today" (Exodus 14:13).

In the book of Job, many accusations, laments, questions, and arguments are thrown around. Eventually, God stepped in and spoke His mind, asking question after question. They are rhetorical questions that have only one realistic and obvious answer: God is in control and has a plan. One of the things God told Job was to stand still. "Listen to this, O Job; stand still and consider the wondrous works of God" (Job 37:14). Then He went on and on about His power and sovereignty.

There is another verse in the Bible that says something quite similar. It is the famous Psalm 46:10: "Be still, and know that I am God; I will be exalted among the nations, I will be exalted in the earth!" All of these verses tell us to *stand still*. What does it mean to stand still? Does it give us permission to do nothing?

Let us look at the specific instructions these verses lay out:

- "Stand still, and *see*" (Exodus 14:13). When the Israelites' enemy came up behind them, and they appeared to be trapped, God wanted them to stop worrying and open their eyes. He wanted them to see—to watch, look, observe, and take note of what He was doing. He wants us to watch and see how He will work. That means placing our eyes on Him and keeping them there so that we do not miss anything, because what He is going to do will be amazing. The next time it appears you are trapped and surrounded by enemies, stop. Stop the progression of fear, stop the thunder of worry, stop the blinding force of doubt, and look to God. He has a plan, so wait on Him!
- "Stand still and *consider*" (Job 37:14). In Job's intense trials, God wanted him to stop talking and start being thoughtful—to think about, contemplate, and reflect on His work. This

lifts the mind to a higher level and turns our depressed thoughts into praise. We are instructed to be in awe of God, who is our Creator and our Savior.

- "Be still, and *know*" (Psalm 46:10). As David waited on God's timing, he responded to God's invitation to get to know Him—to be aware and conscious of His presence and leading and understand that He is God. Building a relationship with God means that we are not only aware that He exists but also that He is Someone we can be familiar with; we can know who He is as our Friend, as our Savior, and as our God.

Standing still is like *waiting on the Lord*. Both phrases tell us not to run ahead of God, fret over what we cannot control, or busy ourselves with the noise of our complaints. In the waiting, in the meantime, there is always a work for us to do, which often includes reaching out and uplifting others who need encouragement and the message of God's love. *Standing still* does not mean idleness; it means that, as we wait for God, we are *watching Him with thoughtfulness and faithfulness.*

Patient trustfulness

In order to wait on the Lord, we need patience and trust. Waiting on the Lord is an expression of trust in God. It means we are confident in His ability to work things out. It means that we have committed to Him the safekeeping of our own lives and the lives of others we may be praying for. It means we have turned the situation over, simply handed it over, to God. *It means that we have let go of the outcome and stopped dictating when and how the particular problems and issues will be resolved. We are letting God's timing become our timing.*

As we learn to wait on God's timing, our eyes are fixed on Him. But this requires patience, as James counsels, "My brethren, count it all joy when you fall into various trials, knowing that the testing of your faith produces patience. But let patience have its perfect work, that you may be perfect and complete, lacking nothing" (James 1:2–4). James teaches us that the testing of our faith produces something very powerful: patience. If we are going to wait on God, we need to be patient with Him and with ourselves. We need to understand that waiting means *accepting delay*. How many times have you prayed for something, and the answer did not seem to come right away? Probably many times. Do not give up. *Wait for it.*

Farming is a good example of patience. "The farmer *waits* for the precious fruit of the earth, *waiting patiently* for it" (James 5:7; emphasis added). It does not do him any good to fret and worry over his field; it will yield fruit (or not) in due time. In a sense, the end result is out of his hands and out of his control. That is a wonderful way to picture the patience we need to exercise while we are waiting for something good. Just as Joseph could not speed up his deliverance from the dungeon by any effort of his own, so the farmer cannot quicken the growth of the seed to produce fruit before its time, no matter what. The plant must develop; the farmer must wait.

Patience is a character trait that often indicates our acceptance and humility in reaction to life's uncertainties and disappointments. When we are patient, we are pliable and expectant. When we are patient, we are trusting in God and, therefore, are calm. *Patience* comes from the Latin verb *pati*, which basically means "to suffer." The Lexico.com dictionary defines *patience* as "the capacity to accept or tolerate delay, trouble, or suffering without getting angry or upset."[1] Imagine that!

Too often, we are chomping at the bit, looking for ways to escape the testing of our faith as quickly as possible. Unfortunately, while in the fire or in prison, anger is often the main emotion that stirs our minds when trials hit. We tend to get so irritated, outraged, and annoyed for having to suffer in any way that we do not allow God to develop patience in us during these trying times. The various trials we fall into test our faith, and the testing of our faith is supposed to produce patience. Romans 5:3 tells us that, ideally, "hardship (distress, pressure, trouble) produces patient endurance" (AMP).

Job's name is right up there near the very top of the list when it comes to suffering at the hands of Satan. That malicious foe killed off Job's entire family, destroyed everything he owned, then caused him to have boils head to toe. His wife, who was dealing with her own grief, told him to "curse God and die" (Job 2:9). And then three of his friends came to him with accusations, misunderstandings, and false doctrines.

Yet James 5:11 tells us, "We count them blessed who endure. You have heard of the perseverance of Job and seen the end intended by the Lord—that the Lord is very compassionate and merciful." Obviously, Job was not a happy man through all of this. Patience and perseverance do not mean having unending happiness this side of heaven.

Job wished that he had never been born. He lamented and grieved his loss. Through it all, he was very honest and straightforward with God. He told God exactly how he felt. He laid out his suffering soul before the Almighty. He asked "why" over and over again, but he never cursed God. In fact, the Bible tells us that through it all, Job did not sin (Job 2:10). He persevered. He endured, even though he did not understand why all the disasters fell upon him.

When the testing of his faith was over,

> the LORD restored Job's losses. . . . Indeed the LORD gave Job twice as much as he had before. . . .
>
> The LORD blessed the latter days of Job more than his beginning (Job 42:10, 12).

And his time of testing has been immortalized for all who come after him, encouraging us that we, too, can persevere even when assaulted by Satan.

In the same way, Joseph patiently endured his trials as a slave and as a wrongfully accused prisoner. He exhibited the patience that we are called to live out—the same patience that Jesus showed us when He "endured the cross" (Hebrews 12:2).

Romans 12:12 counsels, "Rejoicing in hope, patient in tribulation, continuing steadfastly in prayer." Cling to hope, patiently wait for God's deliverance, and never stop praying. Even when we are mistreated, conspired against, and thrown in the dungeon—like Joseph's experience—we are instructed in this verse to be patient in our tribulation and rejoice in hope. Look forward to the day God exalts us and delivers us from our troubles, as He did for both Joseph and Job. Until then, pray. Immediately seek the Lord, be quick to pray, and do not delay. Seek to maintain an ongoing, nonstop conversation with God!

Did you know that there is a day coming when God is going to point to His saints, His people, and say to the whole watching universe, "Here is the *patience* of the saints" (Revelation 14:12; emphasis added)? Here are My people who demonstrate great patience. Can God point to you and say, "Look at how patient he is! Look at how patient she is!"

Until that day arrives, God uses various trials to develop the "*patience of the saints.*" So when we are tried, we are to rejoice that we are being prepared to stand in a time when the writer of Revelation asks, "Who shall be able to stand?" (Revelation 6:17, KJV). Those who have gone through various trials, learned patience and trust, and surrender to God will be the ones who are able to stand!

Let us follow the examples of Joseph, Job, and Jesus, and allow God to cultivate His patience in our lives so that our faith will stand firm at the end. Time spent waiting on God is *never* wasted.

---

1. Lexico.com, s.v. "patience," accessed January 26, 2021, https://www.lexico.com/en/definition/patience.

Chapter 16

In His Power, Amen!

Before we finish Joseph's story, let us look at one final story.

After celebrating the Passover supper, Jesus led His disciples to a place they had visited many times through the years, the Mount of Olives. The birds were singing their evening songs. The sweet smell of spring was in the air, and the sun was setting peacefully, creating a unique silhouette behind the blossoming olive trees. As they walked together, Jesus solemnly told them, "You will all fall away because of Me this night [disillusioned about Me, confused, and some even ashamed of Me]" (Matthew 26:31, AMP). Aghast, they stopped and looked at Him as if to make sure He was really serious. "For it is written," He continued, quoting a prophecy from the prophet Zechariah, " 'I will strike the Shepherd, and the sheep of the flock will be scattered' " (verses 31, 32; compare Zechariah 13:7). His voice brightened for a moment: "But after I have been raised, I will go before you to Galilee" (Matthew 26:32).

We can imagine that the disciples exchanged glances of shock and amazement. Offended and ashamed because of their Lord? Tonight? They had already been through so much with Him. They had followed Jesus faithfully, even amid the growing disgust and ridicule the religious rulers had heaped upon Him. To them, the claim that they would be confused and unfaithful was insulting.

Peter spoke up, "Though all men shall be offended because of You, I will never be offended." His voice rang with conviction and confidence.

Jesus looked at Peter with tender sympathy, but He spoke with gravity and concern. "This night . . . you will deny Me three times."

Peter shook his head forcefully. "Even if I have to die with You, I will not deny You!" The rest of disciples each affirmed the same conviction (verses 34, 35).

"Sit here while I go and pray," Jesus told the disciples (verse 36), and then He signaled for Peter, James, and John to follow Him. They walked in silence. The evening might have been peaceful and restful, but they could sense that Jesus was becoming greatly distressed. His words outlining the events to follow that very night left them feeling agitated and troubled in spirit.

Jesus motioned for the three to stop. He pleaded with them, "Stay here and watch with Me" (verse 38). What He was asking them to do was participate with Him in prayer and watching. Then He walked a little farther.

He could not hold back the growing burden upon Himself. He had never felt such dread and such unease. The climax of His mission—all that He must do and all that He must be—loomed just before Him. He knew the weakness of His human flesh and that it did not have the fortitude to accomplish the impending task. He feared He could so easily fail, and all would be lost. The entire salvation of the human race depended upon Him fulfilling His mission as their Savior. Never had such weight, pressure, and trial been placed on a human being! In this dark time, Jesus recognized His desperate need. He recognized with clarity His frailty. Luke 22:44 tells us, "Being in agony, He prayed more earnestly. Then His sweat became like great drops of blood falling down to the ground."

"Father!" Falling to His knees in agony of His soul. "O My Father!" He whispered, "If You are willing, remove this cup from Me." His humanity shrank from the weight of trial. Yet He gritted His teeth in determination, "Nevertheless, not as I will, but as You will" (Matthew 26:39). He knew that the success of the holy mission depended upon a complete surrender to the will and power of His Father—anything less would mean complete failure. And so, knowing this, He bowed in complete surrender.

Finding His disciples asleep, His heart grieved for them. He did not want to see them overcome and defeated by temptation. So He urged them, specifically speaking to Peter, who had been so assured of himself, "Watch and pray, lest you enter into temptation. The spirit indeed is willing, but the flesh is weak" (verse 41). The message from Jesus to Peter was a loving warning: "Peter, you are weaker than you think. Seek God's help now, before temptations and trials come." Sadly, instead of surrendering themselves to prayer and watchfulness, they surrendered to the pull of sleep.

Soon afterward, the night erupted with trouble and trial. All the disciples fled, just as Jesus had foretold. And Peter denied his Lord three times.

The disciples' supposed strength and passionate devotion quickly vanished, and their words of commitment were forgotten in the chaos of the moment. The prophet Jeremiah reminds us that "the heart is deceitful above all things, and desperately wicked . . . [but] I, the LORD, search the heart" (Jeremiah 17:9, 10). In other words, our hearts tend to lean selfishly toward the wrong things and deceive us, but God understands the detailed, inner workings of why we do what we do, and He wants to tell us the truth about ourselves.

Too often we think that we are just fine, especially if we are going through a time of smooth sailing. Sometimes we know we need to trust God more and pray more often, but we fail to do those very things because we do not *feel* like we need to. It is at such times that we especially need to take heed of Jesus' words: "Watch and pray!"

Trust the One who knows the future

I think it is safe to say that most of us have been in situations that surprised us, caught us off guard, flew out of control, or left us bewildered. Events can happen so fast that we do not even know what hit us. How many times has sudden calamity left us standing utterly confused and defeated when five minutes before we felt like we could conquer the world? Perhaps if we had been spiritually prepared, the outcome would have been vastly different!

The truth is, we do not know what trouble is going to hit us next or when. Remember Joseph? He went from being his father's favorite to being sold as a slave, then after he had proven himself to be a valuable worker and was placed in charge of everything his master owned, he was wrongfully accused and sent to prison. In the same way, we do not know whether trouble will come from our left or right, from behind us, or right smack in front of us. But there is Someone who does know. Jesus knows what lies ahead, and He knows how to equip us to stand strong in faith through every trial that comes our way.

Have you ever found that you have trusted the wrong person, idea, or thing? We are often tempted to do this: the rock looked sturdy enough, the tree limb looked strong enough, the log looked wide enough, or the path looked smooth enough. This misplaced trust comes from relying our own judgment or assumptions instead of on God's perfect insights. Jeremiah likens those who trust in the flesh (themselves or others) to a dead shrub in a salty, uninhabited wilderness (Jeremiah 17:6). When we trust in the flesh, we inevitably depart from trusting God, the Life-Giver. Faith placed in ourselves leads to nothing but empty promises and ropes of sand. Jeremiah 17:7, 8 continues,

> "Blessed is the man who trusts in the LORD,
> And whose hope is the LORD.
> For he shall be like a tree planted by the waters,
> Which spreads out its roots by the river,
> And will not fear when heat comes;
> But its leaf will be green,
> And will not be anxious in the year of drought,
> Nor will cease from yielding fruit."

The difference is striking between the one who trusts in the flesh and the one who trusts in God: the one who trusts in the flesh is dead and dry, while the one who trusts in God is living and strong. Only God knows our true condition, and it is always best to trust Him, even when we feel strong. The people in Jeremiah's day did not feel the need to seek God and trust Him, but the truth was, their own hearts were deceiving them as well.

Jesus had warned Peter that he did not really know his true condition and that he should pray for strength. But he did not feel a deep need for fervent prayer about his condition or for strength to overcome any future temptations. He felt that he was strong enough to overcome on his own. But the truth was, he was terribly weak and vulnerable to the enemy's clever attacks. Oh, my friends, such is our case as well! Proverbs 14:12 says, "There is a way that seems right to a man, but its end is the way of death." Our hearts tend to deceive us, and that is why we *cannot follow our hearts*. Instead, we *must follow God's heart* and heed His counsel.

Connected to the Creator

In this book, we have seen that Jesus warned us that trouble and trial will always be part of our lives in this world. We have seen how God's path sometimes leads us through dark valleys, blazing fires, and prison cells. On our own, we are not strong enough to meet these trials. In order to overcome the trials we face, we must remain persistently faithful to God. Think about the lessons we have learned from the lives of Joseph, Job, David, and Daniel: God sees the future, He encourages us, He provides for our spiritual needs, He knows our hearts, He understands our true spiritual condition, He gives us counsel, and He tells us the truth.

Although God is not physically with us, He has promised to be with us through His Holy Spirit. Before He was arrested, Jesus promised the disciples that He would send the Holy Spirit. "And I will pray the Father, and He will give you another Helper, that He may abide with you forever—the Spirit of truth, whom the world cannot receive, because it neither sees Him nor knows Him; but you know Him, for He dwells with you and will be in you. I will not leave you orphans; I will come to you" (John 14:16–18). It is His Spirit abiding within us that makes us strong and prepares us to meet the trials ahead.

Jesus told His followers, "I am the true vine, and My Father is the vinedresser. . . . Abide in Me, and I in you. As the branch cannot bear fruit of itself, unless it abides in the vine, neither can you, unless you abide in Me" (John 15:1, 4). If we are to survive life's howling winds and battering hail, we must remain attached to our Creator, the True Vine. His Spirit must abide in us. He is our Sustainer. He is our Helper.

Sometimes when I am trying to understand a word, I like to think in opposites. The opposite of the word *kept* is "thrown away" or "neglected." God does not throw us away or neglect us, rather He keeps us. To be "kept" is an expression of belonging. Jesus redeemed us when He bought us with a price. Therefore, we belong to Him—we are His children. And He desires to *keep* us strong in His power and never let us go. His power secures us, nourishes us, and sustains us, creating a strong connection between us (weak humans) and Him (the all-powerful Creator). His Spirit is powerful and able to make us victorious. If we abide in Him through His Spirit working actively in our lives, His Spirit will *keep* us securely in His hands. "Now to Him who is able to keep you from stumbling, and to present you faultless before the presence of His glory with exceeding joy" (Jude 24).

Strengthened by the Almighty

Only God can take weakness and turn it into strength. Only God can take a prisoner and promote him to second-in-command. Only God can take a persecutor and transform him into an evangelist. Remember Paul's personal testimony? "I take pleasure in infirmities, in reproaches, in needs, in persecutions, in distresses, for Christ's sake. For when I am weak, then I am strong" (2 Corinthians 12:10). These are unusual words; I mean, who would take pleasure in any of these situations? Actually, Paul is not saying that he enjoys suffering, rather he has learned that when they occur, he gets to experience the power of God!

Remember that God's grace is a sure sign that He is on our side. And Paul tells us that God's grace is sufficient for us when we are in trouble (verse 9). God is more than enough! We do not need to look anywhere else when trials and temptations come. We may be weak, but we have access to God's throne, and the One who abides within us is the One who has unlimited power and grace to save us.

As a prisoner, Joseph was weak—he could not even defend himself against the false charges against him! So he entrusted his future to the One who knew the truth of what happened. And in trusting God, Joseph became a vehicle for God's grace and strength to be revealed (Genesis 41–45, 47, 50).

We have a sense of calm when we admit that we are weak and cannot overcome on our own. This peace in the soul opens the door to experiencing God's strength and power. This peace fills our mouths with praise. Like Paul and Joseph, the psalmists were not ashamed to admit that they were weak. In Psalm 73:26, Asaph says, "My flesh and my heart fail; but God is the strength of my heart and my portion forever." Another psalmist, a son of Korah, was convinced that "God [was his] refuge and strength, a very present help in trouble" (Psalm 46:1). "A very *present* help" means that God is working in the present. He is available. He is standing by. Through His Spirit, He is willing and ready to help.

Jesus "became flesh and dwelt among us" (John 1:14). He experienced the weaknesses of our human flesh. He experienced the pull of temptation and the weight of trial. But His success rested in the fact that He never relied upon Himself. He knew He was not strong enough *in the flesh* to fight the enemy, overcome evil, and accomplish His mission. He said, "I can of Myself do nothing. . . . I do not seek My own will but the will of the Father who sent Me" (John 5:30). *His continual reliance on His Father was the reason He was successful.* Jesus showed us that *we* can lean upon the strength of God *in all we do*, just as He, our Example, did. After Jesus accomplished His mission, He rose triumphantly and sat at the right hand of His Father in heaven, and now we can look to Him for help.

Empowered and victorious

The Bible continually reinforces this truth: *God wants us to win. He wants us to overcome.* He knows we fall and make mistakes. His desire is to provide us with everything we need to get up and keep moving forward. In a very real sense, we are at war. We are engaged in spiritual warfare with the enemy of our souls. Paul counsels, "Be strong in the Lord and in the power of His might. Put on the whole armor of God, that you may be able to stand against the wiles of the devil" (Ephesians 6:10, 11). We are not left weak and defenseless; instead, God promises that His mighty power will fight alongside us in the battle.

I love how the prophet Micah describes the help God promises us:

Do not rejoice over me, my enemy;
When I fall, I will arise;
When I sit in darkness,
The LORD will be a light to me (Micah 7:8).

We are not meant to be defeated but victorious. We are not meant to walk in darkness but in the light of our God. We do not have to face anything without Him.

I admit that I take no pleasure in tests or trials—at all! How many of us feel the same way? I have found myself praying, "Lord, if it be possible, let me have a strong faith, grow spiritually, and learn all the lessons I need to learn with relative ease." But the reality is that a life of comfort and ease *never* produces a strong soldier. Such a life *never* creates a trusting child. In that place of comfort and ease, there is no feeling of *needing* God or faith.

Reliance, perseverance, patience, and trust are never learned in an environment free from the tough tests and trials of life. It is within the storms and the fires of life that we truly get an opportunity to realize our need of the all-sufficient God. It is in the most troubling times that we may become open and willing to seek His wisdom and guidance. It is when experiencing affliction and adversity that we are given the opportunity to more fully understand His untiring love and care for us. "Shall we indeed accept good from God, and shall we not accept adversity?" (Job 2:10).

Job encourages us to remember, "He knows the way that I take;

when He has tested me, I shall come forth as gold" (Job 23:10). When we go through the raging fires of life, we are refined and purified of the dross that has marred our characters (1 Peter 1:6–9). God has designed that as we come out on the other side of affliction, we possess a greater faith, a stronger trust, a deeper love, a purer heart, and a fiercer hold on our Savior.

At just the right time, God sent dreams to Pharaoh that only His servant Joseph could interpret. At long last, the prison doors swung open, and Joseph began the mission that God had been preparing him for—the mission of saving Egyptians and everyone who came seeking food during the famine, including his own family! Through learning patience and perseverance, God empowered Joseph to fulfill His plan and caused him to be victorious in everything he set his hand to.

At the very beginning of this book, I recounted the experience of Horatio Spafford, who penned the beautiful hymn 'It Is Well With My Soul." His life, like many of our lives, was, no doubt, filled with joys but also with much pain, many tears, and severe trials. Yet in spite of all that he suffered, Horatio could say that whatever his lot, whatever happened, God was his very present help in trouble. Amid the grief, sorrow, and turbulent storms of life, he had found that God had given him every reason to rely upon His Word.

Like Joseph, sudden calamities may seem to disrupt our journeys and make continuing on seem impossible, but Jesus never promised smooth sailing. He may lead us into dark valleys, lions' dens, floods, and blazing fires. Sometimes He permits tragedy and adversity to come our way. He always allows us to exercise free will and experience the consequences of our choices, whether good or bad. But through it all, God promises to be a reliable and faithful Savior, full of power and love. *Our success through the storms of life is dependent on a deep, thriving relationship with Jesus.*

In conclusion, allow me to switch from the plural *we* to the more personal *you*. Perhaps you are in a dark place now. Perhaps the sea you are crossing is wild with boisterous wind. Perhaps your relaxing day is about to erupt with troubles yet unknown. God is pleading with you to allow the experiences of Moses, Joseph, Daniel, Jesus, and everyone we have studied to challenge how you may have viewed stormy seas in the past and how you will react to them in the future. Prayerfully look to God, and see Him as a Savior eager to help you. Take Jesus' outstretched hand right away. Do not delay. He is waiting to help you through any storm you are in and through any storm heading your way.